'DOWRY PROHIBITION ACT 1961' – SUPREME COURT'S LATEST CASE LAWS

CASE NOTES- FACTS- FINDINGS OF APEX COURT JUDGES & CITATIONS

JAYPRAKASH BANSILAL SOMANI

All the Past & Present Judges of the Supreme Court of India.

Salute to their wisdom.

Salute to their interpretation of Law.

Salute to their elaborative judgement writing.

Supreme Court Of India.

Contents

Preface   *vii*

Acknowledgements   *ix*

1. Arun Singh And Ors. Vs. State Of U.P. And Ors. (10.02.2020 - SC) : MANU/SC/0160/2020   1

2. Bobbili Ramakrishna Raju Yadav And Ors. Vs. State Of Andhra Pradesh And Ors. (19.01.2016 - SC) : MANU/SC/0046/2016   4

3. Modinsab Kasimsab Kanchagar Vs. State Of Karnataka And Ors. (11.03.2013 - SC) : MANU/SC/0237/2013   8

4. Biswajit Halder And Ors. Vs. State Of West Bengal (19.03.2007 - SC) : MANU/SC/1480/2007   12

5. Union Of India (UOI) And Ors. Vs. Santosh Kumar Singh (26.04.2023 - SC) : MANU/SC/0480/2023   15

6. Mirza Iqbal And Ors. Vs. State Of Uttar Pradesh And Ors. (14.12.2021 - SC) : MANU/SC/1256/2021   18

7. Parvati Devi Vs. The State Of Bihar And Ors. (17.12.2021 - SC) : MANU/SC/1280/2021   21

8. P XXX Vs. State Of Uttarakhand And Ors. (16.06.2022 - SC) : MANU/SC/0784/2022   24

9. Naresh Kumar Mangla Vs. Anita Agarwal And Ors. (17.12.2020 - SC) : MANU/SC/0951/2020   29

10. Nallapareddy Sridhar Reddy Vs. The State Of Andhra Pradesh And Ors. (21.01.2020 - SC) : MANU/SC/0057/2020   33

11. Sonu Vs. Sonu Yadav And Ors. (05.04.20- SC) : MANU /SC/0243/2021   37

12. Nathu Singh And Ors. Vs. State Of Uttar Pradesh And Ors. (28.05.2021 - SC) : MANU/SC/0360/2021   40

13. Parvez Noordin Lokhandwalla Vs. State Of Maharashtra And Ors. (01.10.2020 - SC) : MANU/SC/0743/2020   43

Contents

14. Preet Pal Singh Vs. The State Of Uttar Pradesh And Ors. (14.08.2020 - SC) : MANU/SC/0591/2020 — 48

15. Charan Singh Vs. The State Of Uttarakhand (20.04.2023 - SC) : MANU/SC/0421/2023 — 52

16. Devender Singh And Ors. Vs. The State Of Uttarakhand (21.04.2022 - SC) : MANU/SC/0517/2022 — 55

17. State Of Madhya Pradesh Vs. Jogendra And Ors. (11.01.2022 - SC) : MANU/SC/0027/2022 — 59

18. Jatinder Kumar Vs. State Of Haryana (17.12.2019 - SC) : MANU/SC/1755/2019 — 62

19. Kantilal Vs. The State Of Gujarat (04.10.2019 - SC) : MANU/SC/1393/2019 — 65

20. Sandeep Kumar And Ors. Vs. State Of Uttarakhand And Ors. (02.12.2020 - SC) : MANU/SC/0910/2020 — 68

21. Arun Singh And Ors. Vs. State Of U.P. And Ors. (10.02.2020 - SC) : MANU/SC/0160/2020 — 71

Adv. Jayprakash Somani's Videos on Law — 75

List of Adv. Jayprakash Somani's Published Books — 81

Adv Jayprakash Somani's Online Courses — 85

Preface

Dear Learned Advocates ofTrial Court, High court and Supreme Court, Corporate and Individuals.

I am very delighted to provide you a book on'DOWRY PROHIBITION ACT 1961'- SUPREME COURT'S LATEST LEADING CASE LAWs

In this book you will get...

1. Name of the Case i. e. Cause title

2.Relevant Sections discussed in the case

3. Hon'ble Judges/Coram of the case

4.Number of PDF Pages in Original Judgement of the case

5. All available Citations of the case

6. Case Note with appeal allowed/ dismissed or disposed off

7. Facts of the case

8. Hon'ble Apex Court's findings, while dismissing/allowing or disposing the appeal

9. Ratio Decidendi if any.

My special thanks to Manupatra, because of their web portal I can compile this book in well manner. I am also thankful to Notion Press to support me to publish & market this book throughout the Country. Thanks to my Juniors, Advocate Colleagues & Insolvency Professional Colleagues to support me in this venture.

Adv. Manoj Kumar Chowdhary & Miss. Pooja Rai has helped me a lot to compile this book. I hope this book will add some value addition in the wealth of your legal knowledge. Your positive feedbacks will boost me to compile/ write further books & negative feedbacks will improve my skills. Kindly send your valuable feedbacks by email.

Thanks with Regards,

Jayprakash B. Somani

Advocate, Supreme Court of India

Email: jaysomani64@gmail.com

Web Site:www.jayprakashsomani.com

Call: 9322188701, 8459194576

Acknowledgements

Printed & Published by
Notion Press
No. 8, 3rd Cross Street,
CIT Colony, Mylapore,
Chennai, Tamil Nadu- 600004
Managed by
Jayprakash Somani Advocates & Solicitors
Law Firm for Supreme Court of India
Delhi Office
B- 851, 1st Floor, Shivaji Marg, New Ashok Nagar, Delhi 110096.
Call: 9322188701, 8459194576
Supreme Court Chamber
312, 3rd Floor, M. C. Setalvad Block, In front of 'D' Gate, Bhagwan Das
Road, Supreme Court of India, New Delhi 110001
Contact: 8459194576, 9811011747
www.jayprakashsomani.com
Download our app to get access to our Free Videos, Free Bare Acts,
Free Study Material in Legal as well as International Business Regime.
Android App Link ;-https://clpandrea.page.link/cmSm
Ios APp Link :-https://apps.apple.com/us/app/classplus/id1324522260
Login with org code ;- (qywzji)
Web Link ;-https://qywzji.courses.store/
Opportunity for Lawyers/ Social Workers to get Supreme Court Law
Firm JSAS's authorised centre at District Level.
Kindly Message or Call to: 9322188701
Books are available online in India
1.Notion Press:https://notionpress.com/author/jayprakash_somani
2.Amazon:https://www.amazon.in/s?k=jayprakash+somani
3.Flipkart:https://www.flipkart.com/search?q=Jayprakash%20Somani
Books are available online at International Market
4. Amazon International: https://www.amazon.com/
s?k=jayprakash+somani
5. Amazon United Kingdom: https://www.amazon.co.uk/
s?k=jayprakash+somani

6. E-Books/Kindle edition at National & International Level: https://www.amazon.in/s?k=jaypraksh+somani

Arun Singh and Ors. vs. State of U.P. and Ors. (10.02.2020 - SC) : MANU/SC/0160/2020

Relative Section:

Code of Criminal Procedure, 1973 (CrPC) - Section 156(3), Code of Criminal Procedure, 1973 (CrPC) - Section 320, Code of Criminal Procedure, 1973 (CrPC) - Section 482; Dowry Prohibition Act, 1961 - Section 3, Dowry Prohibition Act, 1961 - Section 3(1), Dowry Prohibition Act, 1961 - Section 4, Dowry Prohibition Act, 1961 - Section 8(2); Indian Penal Code, 1860 (IPC) - Section 493

Hon'bleJudges/Coram:

Navin Sinha and Krishna Murari, JJ.

Equivalent Citation: 2020(213)AIC73, AIR2020SC1758, 2020 (2) ALD(Crl.) 444 (SC), 2020 (113) ACC 257, 2020(4)Crimes85(SC), 2020(1)HLR888, 2020/INSC/163, 2020(2)J.L.J.R.4, 2020(2)KLT83, 2020-2-LW(Crl)957, 2020(2)PLJR4, 2020(3)RLW2394(SC), (2020)3SCC736, 2020 (5) SCJ 683, [2020]3SCR707

NumberofPagesintheOriginalJudgment: 10

Case Reference:

Gian Singh v. State of Punjab and Anr. MANU/SC/0781/2012; Parbatbhai Aahir and Ors. v. State of Gujarat and Ors. MANU/SC/1241/ 2017; Narinder Singh and Ors. v. State of Punjab and Anr. MANU/SC/ 0235/2014; Ram Chandra Bhagat v. State of Jharkhand MANU/SC/1024/ 2012; Amrawati and Anr. v. State of U.P. MANU/UP/0819/2004 : 2004 (57)

ALR 290; Lal Kamlendra Pratap Singh v. State of U.P. MANU/ SC/ 0449 2009 : 2009 (3) ADJ 322 (SC)

Case Note:

Criminal - Quashing of proceedings - Section 493 of Indian Penal Code, 1860 and Section 3/4 of Dowry Prohibition Act, 1961 - Respondent No. 2 lodged First Information Report under Section 493 of Code read with Section 3/4 of Dowry Prohibition Act against Appellants - Matter was investigated and charge sheet was filed against Appellants, which was challenged before High Court by way of petition - High Court finding that there was no justification for quashing charge sheet dismissed petition - Hence, present appeal - Whether impugned criminal proceedings initiated against Appellants liable to be quashed.

Facts:

The Respondent No. 2 lodged First Information Report with Police Station under Section 493 Indian Penal Code read with Section 3/4 of the Dowry Prohibition Act against the Appellants. The matter was investigated by the concerned Police Station and a charge sheet was filed against the Appellants, which was challenged before the High Court by way of petition under Section 482 Code of Criminal Procedure. The High Court finding that there was no justification for quashing the charge sheet dismissed the petition.

Held, while partly allowing the appeal:

(i) To constitute an offence under Section 493 Indian Penal Code, the allegations in the FIR must demonstrate that Appellant had practiced deception on the daughter of the complainant causing a false belief of existence of lawful marriage and which led her to cohabit with him. [22]

(ii) From a perusal of the F.I.R., there was no allegations made therein could be said to constitute any offence under Section 493 Indian Penal Code. There were no allegation of any inducement or any deceit to make the victim believe that she was lawfully married to the Appellant, which mislead her to have sexual intercourse with the Accused Appellant No. 1. Only allegations in the First Information Report in this regard were that after the marriage was settled, the Appellant No. 1 started visiting the house of the complainant frequently and would mislead and instigate his daughter that relation is final and only Feras remains to be performed. On the fateful day, the Appellant No. 1 took leave and enticed and instigated his daughter took her to his room and promising that she was being his wife established physical relations. [23]

(iii) A perusal of the averments would go to show that ingredients to constitute an offence under Section 493 Indian Penal Code are missing from the averments. The allegations did not even prima-facie, cull out any inducement of belief in the victim that she was lawfully married to the Appellant No. 1 and on account of this deceitful misstatement, the victim co-habited with the Accused. Since the essential ingredients to constitute an offence under Section 493 Indian Penal Code were missing from the allegations made in the F.I.R., offence under the said Section could not be said to be made out against the Appellants. [24]

(iv) A reading of the Section 3/4 of Act shows that essential ingredients of the offence under Section 3/4 of the Dowry Prohibition Act are that the persons Accused should have made demand directly or indirectly from the parents or other relatives or guardians of a bride or a bridegroom as the case may be any dowry and/or abets the giving and taking of dowry. The allegations of the F.I.R. quoted hereinabove clearly go to show that a demand of dowry was made by the Appellants from the complainants and thus it could not be said that no offence under the Dowry Prohibition Act are made out against the Appellants. There being direct allegations of demand of Dowry in the First Information Report, the allegations prima-facie constitute a commission of an offence under the Dowry Prohibition Act and thus the charges leveled against the Appellants under Section 3/4 of the said Act, were not liable to be quashed. [29]

Disposition: In Favour of State

Bobbili Ramakrishna Raju Yadav and Ors. vs. State of Andhra Pradesh and Ors. (19.01.2016 - SC) : MANU/ SC/0046/2016

Relative Section:

Dowry Prohibition Act, 1961 - Section 3, Dowry Prohibition Act, 1961 - Section 4, Dowry Prohibition Act, 1961 - Section 6, Dowry Prohibition Act, 1961 - Section 6(1), Dowry Prohibition Act, 1961 - Section 6(3); Indian Penal Code, 1860 (IPC) - Section 304B, Indian Penal Code, 1860 (IPC) - Section 405, Indian Penal Code, 1860 (IPC) - Section 406, Indian Penal Code, 1860 (IPC) - Section 498A; Code of Criminal Procedure, 1973 (CrPC) - Section 482

Hon'bleJudges/Coram:

T.S. Thakur, C.J.I., A.K. Sikri and R. Banumathi, JJ.

Equivalent Citation:

2016(1)ACR853, 2016(159)AIC264, AIR2016SC442, AIR2016SC442, 2016(1)AJR817, 2016 (1) ALD(Crl.) 361 (SC) , 2016 (93) ACC 503, 2016(1)BomCR(Cri)826, I(2016)CCR335(SC), 121(2016)CLT486, 2016CriLJ 1141, 2016CriLJ1141, 2016(1)Crimes142(SC), I(2016)DMC374SC, 2016(1)ECrN 700, 2016/INSC/60, 2016(1)J.L.J.R.454, 2016(2)JCC826, 2016-2-LW(Crl)358, 2016(1)MLJ(Crl)519, 2016(2)N.C.C.400, 2016(I)OLR594, 2016(2)PLJR57, (2016)1PLR799,

(2016)181PLR799, 2016(1)RCR(Criminal)853, 2016(2)RLW1005(SC), 2016(1)SCALE350, (2016)3SCC309, 2016 (3) SCJ 310, [2016]1SCR103, 2016(1)UC239, 2016 (1) WLN 225 (SC)

NumberofPagesintheOriginalJudgment: 7

Case Reference:

Pratibha Rani v. Suraj Kumar and Anr. MANU/SC/0090/1985 : (1985) 2 SCC 370; Madhavrao Jiwajirao Scindia and Ors. v. Sambhajirao Chandrojirao Angre and Ors. MANU/SC/0261/1988 : (1988) 1 SCC 692

Case Note:

Criminal - Returning of dowry - Dowry death - Marriage of first Appellant performed with Syamala Rani - Syamala Rani died under mysterious circumstances - Case registered under Sections 304B, 498A Indian Penal Code - Read with Sections 3 and 4 Dowry Prohibition Act - Chargesheet filed against Appellant 1 to 6 - Case committed to Sessions Court - Second Respondent-father of Syamala Rani filed private complaint - Against Appellants - Under Section 6 of Dowry Prohibition Act - Alleged - He had paid dowry amount and other articles were presented as dowry - Same were not returned - Magistrate took cognizance of offence under Section 6 - Appellants preferred petition Under Section 482 Code of Criminal Procedure - Quash the complaint - Contended that complaint does not disclose an offence - FIR was already registered - High Court dismissed petition filed by Appellants - Held - Offences alleged in previous case emanating from FIR and subsequent complaint - Not the same -Appellants preferred present Appeal - Whether the dowry was given to Appellants 2 to 6 and that they were duty bound to return the same to Syamala Rani - Whether continuation of criminal proceedings against Appellants 2 to 6 is just and proper

Facts:

First Appellant is working as an Engineer in G.E. India Technology Company at Bangalore. Appellants No. 2 and 3 are the parents, Appellant No. 4 is widowed sister and Appellants No. 5 and 6 are the sisters of Appellant No. 1. Marriage of first Appellant and Syamala Rani was performed at Vizianagaram and after marriage, Syamala Rani was residing at Bangalore with her husband-Appellant No. 1. Syamala Rani died under suspicious circumstances and a case was registered Under Sections 304B, 498A Indian Penal Code read with Sections 3 and 4 of the Dowry Prohibition Act.

On completion of investigation in the said case, chargesheet was filed against the Appellants No. 1 to 6 and the case was committed to Sessions Court and was taken on file in the Court of Principal Sessions Judge, Bangalore. Second Respondent-father of Syamala Rani filed a private complaint against the Appellants Under Section 6 of the Dowry Prohibition Act alleging that he had paid dowry amount and other articles which were presented as dowry to the Appellants on their demand and the same were not returned. The Magistrate took cognizance of the offence Under Section 6 of the Dowry Prohibition Act.

The Appellants then preferred a petition Under Section 482 Code of Criminal Procedure before the High Court to quash the complaint contending that the complaint does not disclose an offence and that FIR was already registered against the Appellants at Bangalore city. The High Court vide the impugned order dismissed the petition filed by the Appellants holding that the offences alleged in the previous case emanating from the FIR and the subsequent complaint are not one and the same as the previous case was registered Under Sections 304B and 498A Indian Penal Code read with Sections 3 and 4 of the Dowry Prohibition Act, whereas the subsequent case is registered Under Section 6 of the Dowry Prohibition Act which is independent of the previous case. Being aggrieved, the Appellants have preferred this appeal.

Held, while partly allowing the appeal

1. Section 6 of the Dowry Prohibition Act lays down that where the dowry is received by any person other than the bride, that person has to transfer the same to the woman in connection with whose marriage it is given and if he fails to do so within three months from the date of the marriage, he shall be punished for violation of Section 6 of the Dowry Prohibition Act.[8]

2. If the dowry amount or articles of married woman was placed in the custody of his husband or in-laws, they would be deemed to be trustees of the same. The person receiving dowry articles or the person who is dominion over the same, as per Section 6 of the Dowry Prohibition Act, is bound to return the same within three months after the date of marriage to the woman in connection with whose marriage it is given. If he does not do so, he will be guilty of a dowry offence under this Section.[9]

3. It is seen that there is no specific allegations against Appellants 2 to 6 that the dowry articles were entrusted to them and that they have not returned the dowry amount and the articles to Syamala Rani. Equally,

there are no allegations that those dowry articles were kept in Vizianagaram and used by Appellants 2 to 6 who were separately living away from the couple in Bangalore. Even though complainant has alleged that the dowry amount was paid at the house of the accused at Gajapathinagaram, there are no specific allegations of entrustment of the dowry amount and articles to Appellants 2 to 6.[12]

4. Giving of dowry and the traditional presents at or about the time of wedding does not in any way raise a presumption that such a property was thereby entrusted and put under the dominion of the parents-in-law of the bride or other close relations so as to attract ingredients of Section 6 of the Dowry Prohibition Act. As noticed earlier, after marriage, Syamala Rani and first Appellant were living in Bangalore at their matrimonial house. In respect of 'stridhana articles' given to the bride, one has to take into consideration the common practice that these articles are sent along with the bride to her matrimonial house. It is a matter of common knowledge that these articles are kept by the woman in connection with whose marriage it was given and used by her in her matrimonial house when the Appellants 2 to 6 have been residing separately in Vizianagaram, it cannot be said that the dowry was given to them and that they were duty bound to return the same to Syamala Rani.[13]

5. Facts and circumstances of the case and also the uncontroverted allegations made in the complaint do not constitute an offence Under Section 6 of the Dowry Prohibition Act against Appellants 2 to 6 and there is no sufficient ground for proceeding against the Appellants 2 to 6. Be it noted that Appellants 2 to 6 are also facing criminal prosecution for the offence Under Sections 498A, 304B Indian Penal Code and Under Sections 3 and 4 of the Dowry Prohibition Act. Even though the criminal proceeding Under Section 6 of the Dowry Prohibition Act is independent of the criminal prosecution Under Sections 3 and 4 of Dowry Prohibition Act, in the absence of specific allegations of entrustment of the dowry amount and articles to Appellants 2 to 6, in Court's view, continuation of the criminal proceeding against Appellants 2 to 6 is not just and proper and the same is liable to be quashed.[13]

6. The impugned order in Criminal Petition No. 1778 of 2010 is set aside qua the Appellants 2 to 6 and the appeal is partly allowed.[14]

Modinsab Kasimsab Kanchagar vs. State of Karnataka and Ors. (11.03.2013 - SC) : MANU/SC/ 0237/2013

Relative Section:

Dowry Prohibition Act, 1961 - Section 2, Dowry Prohibition Act, 1961 - Section 3, Dowry Prohibition Act, 1961 - Section 4, Dowry Prohibition Act, 1961 - Section 5(1), Dowry Prohibition Act, 1961 - Section 6; Indian Penal Code 1860, (IPC) - Section 304B; Indian Penal Code 1860, (IPC) - Section 34; Section 498A

Hon'bleJudges/Coram:

A.K. Patnaik and S.J. Mukhopadhaya, JJ.

Equivalent Citation:

2013(125)AIC185, AIR2013SC1504, 2013(2) AKR 366, 2013(1)ALD(Cri)971, 2013 (81) ACC 978, 2013Bom CR(Cri)638, 2013(2)BomCR(Cri)638, II(2013)CCR236(SC), 2013CriLJ2056, 2013(3)Crimes255(SC), 2013(3) ECrN 698, 2013(1)HLR590, 2013(2)JCC992, JT2013(4)SC41, 2013(4)KarLJ564, 2013(4)KCCR2625, 2013 (4) MPHT416, (2013)170PLR665, (2013)2PLR665, 2013(2)RCR(Criminal)446, 2013(3)SCALE443, (2013) 4SCC551, [2013]2SCR357

NumberofPagesintheOriginalJudgment: 6

Case Reference:

Appasaheb and Anr. v. State of Maharashtra MANU/SC/7002/2007 : (2007) 9 SCC 721

Case Note:

Criminal - Conviction - Challenge thereto - Sections 498A and 304B of Indian Penal Code 1860; Sections 3, 4 and 6 of Dowry Prohibition Act, 1961 - High Court reversed order of Trial Court only qua Appellant/husband and convicted Appellant for offences punishable under Sections 498A and 304B and Sections 3, 4 and 6 of Act - Hence, this Appeal - Whether High Court was justified to reverse order of Trial Court - Held, sum of 1000 in cash and one tola of gold in addition to other articles were given to Appellant at time of marriage towards dowry - Section 3(1) of Act clearly intended to exempt presents which were given at time of marriage to bride or bride groom from prohibition against dowry under Act - Thereby, Trial Court might have taken view that if anything was given to Appellant in form of "Varopachara" such payment might not attract provisions of Act - However, High Court found that Appellant was guilty of offences under Sections 3, 4 and 6 of Act but had not considered offences to be grave and imposed punishments for only six months for each of offences in accordance with proviso to Section 5(1) of Act - Therefore considering lenient view taken by High Court of offences under Act, no interference was needed with findings of High Court - Hence, conviction of Appellant under Section 304B of IPC was set aside and conviction of Appellant under Section 498A of IPC and under Act was maintained - Appeal allowed.

Ratio Decidendi :"Courts hall not interfere with findings of Lower Courts unless there is certain error apparent on face of record "

Facts:

The facts very briefly are:[2]

2.1 The Appellant was married to Rajbee on 21st April, 1997. She committed suicide on 29th March, 1998. A case was registered and investigated by the Police Inspector [Anti-Dowry Cell] and charge sheet was filed against the Appellant and the mother of the Appellant for offences under Sections 498A and 304B read with Section 34 Indian Penal Code as well as Sections 3, 4 and 6 of the Dowry Prohibition Act read with Section 34 of Indian Penal Code.

2.2 The prosecution case was that at the time of marriage of the Appellant with Rajbee (the deceased), `1,000/- cash and one tola of gold was given to the Appellant and thereafter the Appellant harassed the deceased further for more dowry of `10,000/- and the deceased informed about this harassment to her mother. Thereafter, the mother of the deceased was able to give `2000/- towards the demand but was unable to pay the balance amount of `8000/-. The deceased came along with the Appellant to her mother's place and when the Appellant was told that her family does not have any capacity to meet the balance demand of `8000/-, the deceased went back to her matrimonial house weeping and saying that her life would not be safe. She came back again to her mother's place during the Holi festival and complained of harassment and once again asked for the balance amount of `8000/-, but the same was not paid to her by her mother and within fifteen days of this incident, the deceased committed suicide.

2.3 At the trial, mother of the deceased was examined as P.W. 2 and two of her uncles were examined as P.W. 3 and P.W. 4 and besides them four other witnesses were examined as P. Ws. 5, 7, 10 and 12, who all deposed about the demand of ` 1,000/- cash and one tola of gold as well as demand of `10,000/- and about the fact that `1,000/- cash and one tola of gold were actually given to the Appellant at the time of marriage and also about the fact that out of the demand of `10,000/- made after the marriage, `2,000/- was paid but the balance of `8,000/- could not be paid because of which the deceased was harassed and she committed suicide. Nonetheless, the trial court acquitted the Appellant of the charges by its judgment dated 2nd December, 1999.

2.4 Aggrieved, the State of Karnataka filed Criminal Appeal No. 805 of 2000 before the High Court and by the impugned judgment, the High Court reversed the order of the trial court only qua the Appellant-husband and convicted the Appellant for the offences punishable under Section 498A, 304B and Sections 3, 4 and 6 of the Dowry Prohibition Act and sentenced the Appellant to undergo simple imprisonment for a period of seven years for the offence under Section 304B and in view of the sentence awarded under Section 304B, the High Court did not award any separate sentence for the offence under Section 498A. In respect of the offences under Sections 3, 4 and 6 of the Dowry Prohibition Act, the High Court sentenced the Appellant to undergo simple imprisonment for a period of six months for each of the three offences.

Held, while allowing the appeal

1. In the result, we set aside the conviction of the Appellant under Section 304B Indian Penal Code and the sentence there under but maintain the conviction of the Appellant under Section 498A Indian Penal Code

and under the Dowry Prohibition Act, 1961. We maintain the sentence of six months' imprisonment awarded to the Appellant under the Dowry Prohibition Act for each of the offences under the said Act and award sentence of approximately two years which the Appellant is stated to have already undergone for the offence under Sections 498A Indian Penal Code and further direct that the sentences under Section 498A Indian Penal Code as well as the offences under the Dowry Prohibition Act, 1961 will run concurrently.[11]

2. The appeal is allowed to the aforesaid extent. The bail bonds stand discharged.[12]

CHAPTER FOUR

Biswajit Halder and Ors. vs. State of West Bengal (19.03.2007 - SC) : MANU/ SC/1480/2007

Relative Section:

Dowry Prohibition Act, 1961 - Section 3, Dowry Prohibition Act, 1961 - Section 3(1), Dowry Prohibition Act, 1961 - Section 4; Indian Evidence Act, 1872 - Section 113B; Indian Penal Code 1860, (IPC) - Section 304B; Indian Penal Code 1860, (IPC) - Section 34; Indian Penal Code 1860, (IPC) - Section 498A

Hon'bleJudges/Coram:

Dr. Arijit Pasayat and S.H. Kapadia, JJ.

Equivalent Citation: 2007(2)ACR2341(SC), 2007(2)ALD(Cri)975, 2007(2)ALT(Cri)162, 2007(1)CLJ(SC)286, CLT(2008)Supp.Crl.281, 2007CriLJ2300, I(2007)DMC539SC, 2007GLH(2)78, JT2007(5)SC360, 2007N.C.C.444, RLW2008(1)SC711, 2007(4)SCALE462, (2008)1SCC202, [2007]4SCR120

NumberofPagesintheOriginalJudgment:4

Case Reference:

Smt. Shanti and Anr. v. State of Haryana MANU/SC/0507/1991; **Kanchy Ramchander v. State of A.P.**

Case Note:

Indian Penal Code, 1860 - Section 304B--Dowry death--Ingredients of Section 304B--No evidence to show any cruelty or harassment for or in connection with dowry demand--No finding in that regard--Deficiency in evidence--Fatal to prosecution case--Even otherwise mere evidence of cruelty or harassment--Not sufficient to attract Section 304B--It has to be seen in addition that such cruelty or harassment was for or in connection with demand for dowry--Conviction unsustainable-- And set aside.

The basic ingredients to attract the provisions of Section 304B, I.P.C. are as follows :

(1) The death of a woman should be caused by burns or fatal injury or otherwise than under normal circumstances ;

(2) Such death should have occurred within seven years of her marriage ;

(3) She must have been subjected to cruelty or harassment by her husband or any relative of her husband ; and

(4)Such cruelty or harassment should be for or in connection with demand for dowry.

Ratio Decidendi : "Evidence must prove causing of cruelty or harassment was for or in connection with the demand for dowry absence of which would prove fatal for the prosecution case."

Case Category: CRIMINAL MATTERS - MATTERS RELATING TO HARASSMENT, CRUELTY TO WOMAN FOR DOWRY, DOWRY DEATH, EVE-TEASING, DOMESTIC VIOLENCE ETC.

Facts:

The prosecution version in brief is as follows:[3]

Rupali, sister of informant Dilip Patra (PW-1) was married to appellant Biswajit Hider-appellant No. 1 on 6th March, 1992. Appellants Dulal Chandra Haider and Maya Haider are the parents of Biswajit. At the time of marriage dowry i.e. of Rs. 43,000/ , gold ornaments and the household articles were given to the appellants, but they were not satisfied with the dowry items. Since marriage Rupali was put under pressure to bring one colour television, English Khat and VIP bag for her father-in-law and other relatives, Rupali time and again had reported about the persistent demand of the appellants to her father and brothers. Rupali's brother (PW-1) on different occasions requested the appellants not to harass Rupali for non-payment of those items. On 27th July, 1992 Rupali committed suicide at the house of the appellants by consuming poison and after getting the sad news from his relatives, PW-1, who being a member of Indian Armed Forces was posted at Punjab, came to his native village and lodged the FIR on 6th August, 1992. On receipt of the FIR, police started investigation and on completion of investigation, charge sheet was submitted against the appellants for their trial.

Held, while allowing the appeal

1. In this case we find that there is practically no evidence to show that there was any cruelty or harassment for or in connection with the demand of dowry. There is also no finding in that regard. This deficiency in evidence proves fatal for the prosecution case. Even otherwise mere evidence of cruelty and harassment is not sufficient to bring in application of Section 304B IPC. It has to be shown in addition that such cruelty or harassment was for or in connection with the demand for dowry. (See: Kanchy Ramchander v. State of A.P. . Since the prosecution failed to prove that aspect, the conviction as recorded cannot be maintained.[9]

2. The appeal is allowed. [10]

CHAPTER FIVE

Union of India (UOI) and Ors. vs. Santosh Kumar Singh (26.04.2023 - SC) : MANU/SC/0480/2023

Relative Section:

Dowry Prohibition Act, 1961 - Section 3, Dowry Prohibition Act, 1961 - Section 4; Indian Penal Code, 1860 (IPC) - Section 34, Indian Penal Code, 1860 (IPC) - Section 201, Indian Penal Code, 1860 (IPC) - Section 302, Indian Penal Code, 1860 (IPC) - Section 304B, Indian Penal Code, 1860 (IPC) - Section 498A; Railway Protection Force Rules, 1987 - Rule 52(1), Railway ProtectionForce Rules, 1987 - Rule 52(2), Railway Protection Force Rules, 1987 - Rule 67(2)

Hon'bleJudges/Coram:

Sanjiv Khanna and Aravind Kumar, JJ.

Equivalent Citation: [2023(177)FLR956], 2023/INSC/435, (2023)IILLJ598SC

NumberofPagesintheOriginalJudgment: 5

Case Reference: nil

Case Note:

Service - Discharge - Criminal proceedings - Rules 52.1, 52.2 and 67.2 of Railway Protection Force Rule, 1987 - Respondent was given employment as Constable on compassionate grounds in Force - As per terms of engagement, antecedents of Respondent had to be verified before being formally enrolled and authorities came to know that First Information Report had been registered against Respondent - On receipt of said information and order was passed by which Respondent was discharged from service - On being acquitted, Respondent made representation to Director General, Force, which was not accepted - Thereupon, he preferred writ petition before Single Judge of High Court which stand dismissed by recording that there was substantial delay of over six years in challenging order of discharge - Aggrieved, Respondent preferred intra-court appeal - Division Bench held that as Respondent had been acquitted in criminal trial, his discharge from service would not be valid - Hence, present appeal - Whether there was any legal fault with discharge order of Respondent.

Facts:

The Respondent was given employment as a Constable on compassionate grounds in the Force. The Respondent had filled up the Attestation Form and was permitted to join the training course. As per the terms of engagement, the antecedents of the Respondent had to be verified before being formally enrolled. Accordingly and as required, the authorities had written to the police to verify the antecedents of the Respondent and came to know that First Information Report had been registered against the Respondent. On receipt of the said information and details, by an order/ letter, the Respondent was discharged from service in terms of the Railway Protection Force Rules, 1987.The Respondent did not immediately challenge the discharge order/letter. However, on being acquitted, the Respondent made a representation to the Director General, the Force, which was not accepted. Thereupon, he preferred a writ petitionbefore the Single Judge of the Calcutta High Court. The writ petition was dismissed by the Single Judge recording that there was delay of over six years in challenging the order of discharge. Aggrieved, the Respondent preferred an intra-court appeal. The Division Bench, in the intra-court appeal, had proceeded on the basis that the Respondent had not given false and wrong information in the Attestation Form. As the Respondent had been acquitted in the criminal trial, his discharge from service would not be valid.

Held, while allowing the appeal:

(i) Rules 52.1 and 52.2 of the 1987 Rules show that upon selection of a recruit but before his formal appointment to the Force, his character and antecedents have to be verified as per the procedure prescribed by the Central Government. If, on verification, the recruit is not found to be suitable for the Force, he shall not be appointed. Rule 67.2 of the 1987 Rules states that a direct recruit selected for being appointed as enrolled member, till the time he is not formally appointed to the Force, can be discharged at any stage if the Chief Security Commissioner, for reasons to be recorded in writing, deems it fit in the interest of the Force. It was an accepted case that the Respondent was not formally appointed. It was during the character and antecedents verification exercise that the Respondent's involvement in the criminal case had come to the notice of the authorities. The authorities had, thereupon, in exercise of power under Rules 52.2 and 67.2 of the 1987 Rules, passed an order/letter recording in writing that the Respondent was not deemed to be fit for service in the interest of the Force. The discharge order/letter expressly states that the Respondent had conducted himself in an unbecoming manner and, keeping in view that he was facing serious criminal charges, it was decided to discharge him. In the given facts, it was difficult to find any legal fault with the discharge order/letter. [8]

Disposition: Appeal Allowed

Mirza Iqbal and Ors. vs. State of Uttar Pradesh and Ors. (14.12.2021 - SC) : MANU/SC/ 1256/2021

Relative Section:

Code of Criminal Procedure, 1973 (CrPC) - Section 173(2), Code of Criminal Procedure, 1973 (CrPC) - Section 482; Dowry Prohibition Act, 1961 - Section 3, Dowry Prohibition Act, 1961 - Section 4; Indian Penal Code, 1860 (IPC) - Section 304B, Indian Penal Code, 1860 (IPC) - Section 323, Indian Penal Code, 1860 (IPC) - Section 406, Indian Penal Code, 1860 (IPC) - Section 498A, Indian Penal Code, 1860 (IPC) - Section 504, Indian Penal Code, 1860 (IPC) - Section 506

Hon'bleJudges/Coram:

R. Subhash Reddy and Hrishikesh Roy, JJ.

Equivalent Citation: 2022(1)ACR727, 2022(231)AIC134, AIR2022SC69, 2022 (119) ACC 247, 2022 (1) ALT (Crl.)487(A.P.), 2022(3)BLJ37, (2022)1CALLT54(SC), 133(2022)CLT416, 2021(4)Crimes580(SC), 2022 (1)CriminalCC256, 2022(1)HLR220, 2021/ INSC/890, 2022(1)JKJ26[SC], 2022(2)N.C.C.40, 2022(1) RCR (Criminal)340, [2021]9SCR469, 2022(1)UC196

NumberofPagesintheOriginalJudgment: 5

Case Reference:

Geeta Mehrotra and Ors. v. State of U.P. and Ors. MANU/SC/0895/ 2012; Ramesh and Ors. v. State of Tamil Nadu MANU/SC/0174/2005

Case Note:

Criminal - Quashing of chargesheet - Order of Cognizance - Section 482 of the Code of Criminal Procedure, 1973 (CrPC) - Offences alleged punishable under Sections 304B, 323, 498-A504, 506 of the Indian Penal Code, 1860 (IPC) - Sections 3 and 4 of the Dowry Prohibition Act, 1961 (DP Act) - Appellants contended allegations levelled to be vague and bald and pleaded false implication -Whether the present was the fit case to be quashed and High Court erred in not quashing the chargesheet in question?

Facts.

The offences alleged included dowry demand in form of four-wheeler and cash. Accused were alleged of beating complainant's daughter and killing her by putting a noose around her neck and hanging her. A case was registered against all the named Accused including the Appellants herein, who are brother-in-law and mother-in-law of the deceased for the alleged offences. When the Appellants filed quash petition before the High Court, it was disposed of by impugned order directing the Appellants to surrender before the Court below and apply for grant of bail and the same was directed to be considered in accordance with law. Hence, the present appeal.

Held, while allowing the Appeal:

The Appellants are brother-in-law and mother-in-law respectively of the deceased. A perusal of the complaint filed by the 2nd Respondent, pursuant to which a crime was registered, does not indicate any specific allegations by disclosing the involvement of the Appellants. It is the specific case of the 1st Appellant that he was working as a cashier in ICICI Bank at Khalilabad branch. It was his specific case that during the relevant time, he was working at ICICI Bank, Khalilabad branch, Gorakhpur and his mother was also staying with him. The Branch Manager has endorsed his presence in the branch, showing in-time at 09:49 a.m. and out-time at 06:25 p.m. Even in the statement of 2nd Respondent recorded by the police and also in the final report filed under Section 173(2) of Code of Criminal Procedure, except omnibus and vague allegations, there is no specific allegation against the Appellants to show their involvement for the offences alleged. [11]

Though there is an allegation of causing injuries, there are no other external injuries noticed in the postmortem certificate, except the single ante-mortem injury i.e. ligature mark around the neck, and the cause of death is shown as asphyxia. Having regard to the case of the Appellants and the material placed on record, except vague and bald allegations against the Appellants, there are no specific allegations disclosing the involvement of the Appellants to prosecute them for the offences alleged.[12]

Appeal allowed. Impugned order set aside. Consequently, the charge sheet filed in FIR under Sections 498-A, 323, 504, 506, 304-B of Indian Penal Code and Sections 3 & 4 of the D.P. Act and the consequential order passed by the Chief Judicial Magistrate quashed.[13]

Disposition: In Favour of Accused

Parvati Devi vs. The State of Bihar and Ors. (17.12.2021 - SC) : MANU/SC/1280/2021

Relative Section:

Dowry Prohibition Act, 1961 - Section 2, Dowry Prohibition Act, 1961 - Section 3, Dowry Prohibition Act, 1961 - Section 4; Indian Evidence Act, 1872 - Section 113B; Indian Penal Code, 1860 (IPC) - Section 34, Indian Penal Code, 1860 (IPC) - Section 201, Indian Penal Code, 1860 (IPC) - Section 304, Indian Penal Code, 1860 (IPC) - Section 304B

Hon'bleJudges/Coram:

N.V. Ramana, C.J.I., Surya Kant and Hima Kohli

Equivalent Citation : 2022(231)AIC159, AIR2022SC1268, 2022 (1) ALD(Crl.) 952 (SC), 2022CriLJ1364, 2022(1)Crimes23(SC), 2022(1)CriminalCC18, II(2022)DMC89SC,II(2022)DMC256SC, 2022(1)HLR258, 2021/ INSC/911, 2022(1)J.L.J.R.121, 2022(1)JLJ25, 2022(1)N.C.C.199, 2022(1)PLJR1, 2022(1)RCR(Criminal)509, [2021]9SCR711, 2022(1)UC601

NumberofPagesintheOriginalJudgment: 9

Case Reference:

Bansi Lal v. State of Haryana MANU/SC/0051/2011; Maya Devi and Ors. v. State of Haryana MANU/SC/ 1398 /2015; G.V. Siddaramesh v. State of Karnataka MANU/SC/0088/2010; Ashok Kumar v. State of Haryana MANU/SC/0491/2010

Case Note:

Criminal -Conviction - Sections 304B and 201 read with Section 34 of the Indian Penal Code, 1860 (IPC) -Trial Court convicted Accused Person - High Court concurred with the view of Trial Court - Hence, the present appeal - High Court agreed with trial Court that Accused failed to explain the circumstances under which the deceased had vanished from her matrimonial home –Whether Accused person rightly convicted by Courts below ?

Facts:

Victim in the instant case was alleged of being harassed, brutally assaulted and threatened for not meeting with dowry demands. Till the time deceased victim went missing from her matrimonial home, she stayed last there itself. Trial Court had convicted the accused person. In appeal, linking the chain of circumstances, High Court concurred with the findings of trial court and inculpated all the three accused. Hence the present appeal.

Held, while disposing the Appeals:

In the instant case, despite the shoddy investigation conducted by the prosecution, the circumstances set out in Section 304B of the Indian Penal Code have been established in the light of the fact that the deceased had gone missing from her matrimonial home within a few months of her marriage and immediately after demands of dowry were made on her and that her death had occurred under abnormal circumstances, such a death would have to be characterized as a "dowry death".[18]

Recovery of the body from the banks of the river clearly indicates that she had died under abnormal circumstances that could only be explained by her husband and in-laws, as she was residing at her matrimonial home when she suddenly disappeared and no plausible explanation was offered for her disappearance. [19]

Case of the prosecution rests solely on circumstantial evidence. No eye witness has been produced who could testify as to how the body of the deceased was found on the banks of river Barakar. There were no signs of any ante mortem injury on the body. If the deceased was killed in the house, then the body would certainly have revealed some signs of struggle.[21]

The circumstances put together, unerringly point to his guilt in extinguishing the life of his wife within a few months of the marriage on her failing to satisfy the demands of dowry. The impugned judgment does not deserve interference and is maintained. [22]

As for A-3 (Mother-in-law), from the evidence on record only certain omnibus allegations have been made against her with respect to dowry demands. Appeal filed by A-3 accordingly allowed. She is directed to be released forthwith. [23]

P XXX vs. State of Uttarakhand and Ors. (16.06.2022 - SC) : MANU/ SC/0784/2022

Relative Section:

Code of Criminal Procedure, 1973 (CrPC) - Section 156(2), Code of Criminal Procedure, 1973 (CrPC) - Section 156(3), Code of Criminal Procedure, 1973 (CrPC) - Section 161, Code of Criminal Procedure, 1973 (CrPC) - Section 164, Code of Criminal Procedure, 1973 (CrPC) - Section 177, Code of Criminal Procedure, 1973 (CrPC) - Section 178, Code of Criminal Procedure, 1973 (CrPC) - Section 178(c), Code of Criminal Procedure, 1973 (CrPC) - Section 178(d), Code of Criminal Procedure, 1973 (CrPC) - Section 179, Code of Criminal Procedure, 1973 (CrPC) - Section 180, Code of Criminal Procedure, 1973 (CrPC) - Section 184, Code of Criminal Procedure, 1973 (CrPC) - Section 188, Code of Criminal Procedure, 1973 (CrPC) - Section 208, Code of Criminal Procedure, 1973 (CrPC) - Section 212(2), Code of Criminal Procedure, 1973 (CrPC) - Section 218, Code of Criminal Procedure, 1973 (CrPC) - Section 218(1), Code of Criminal Procedure, 1973 (CrPC) - Section 219, Code of Criminal Procedure, 1973 (CrPC) - Section 219(1), Code of Criminal Procedure, 1973 (CrPC) - Section 220, Code of Criminal Procedure, 1973 (CrPC) - Section 220(1), Code of Criminal Procedure, 1973 (CrPC) - Section 220(3), Code of Criminal Procedure, 1973 (CrPC) - Section 221, Code of Criminal Procedure, 1973 (CrPC) - Section 221(1), Code of Criminal Procedure, 1973 (CrPC) - Section 221(2), Code of Criminal Procedure, 1973 (CrPC)

- Section 223, Code of Criminal Procedure, 1973 (CrPC) - Section 227, Code of Criminal Procedure, 1973 (CrPC) - Section 232, Code of Criminal Procedure, 1973 (CrPC) - Section 258, Code of Criminal Procedure, 1973 (CrPC) - Section 300, Code of Criminal Procedure, 1973 (CrPC) - Section 376, Code of Criminal Procedure, 1973 (CrPC) - Section 461; Constitution of India - Article 20, Constitution of India - Article 20(2); Dowry Prohibition Act, 1961 - Section 3, Dowry Prohibition Act, 1961 - Section 4; General Clauses Act 1897 - Section 26; Indian Evidence Act, 1872 - Section 114A; Indian Penal Code, 1860 (IPC) - Section 34, Indian Penal Code, 1860 (IPC) - Section 71, Indian Penal Code, 1860 (IPC) - Section 90, Indian Penal Code, 1860 (IPC) - Section 304B, Indian Penal Code, 1860 (IPC) - Section 376, Indian Penal Code, 1860 (IPC) - Section 406, Indian Penal Code, 1860 (IPC) - Section 498A, Indian Penal Code, 1860 (IPC) - Section 504, Indian Penal Code, 1860 (IPC) - Section 506

Hon'bleJudges/Coram:

Dinesh Maheshwari and Vikram Nath, JJ.

Equivalent Citation: 2022(236)AIC201, AIR2022SC2885, 2022 (120) ACC 952, 2022(4)BLJ217, 2022(3)BomCR(Cri)8, 2022CriLJ3579, 2022(3)Crimes110(SC), 2022(4)CTC125, 2022/INSC/648, 2022(3)J.L.J.R.396, 2022(6)JKJ158[SC], 2022 (2) MWN (CR.) 408, 2022(3)PLJR373, 2022 (3) RCR (Criminal)599, 2022(3)RLW1876(SC), 2022(3)ShimLC1546, 2022(3)UC1652

NumberofPagesintheOriginalJudgment:21

Case Reference:

Satvinder Kaur v. State (Govt. of N.C.T. of Delhi) and Ors. MANU/SC/0632/1999; State of Punjab v. Gurmit Singh and Ors. MANU/SC/0366/1996; Sunita Kumari Kashyap v. State of Bihar and Ors. MANU /SC /0402/ 2011; Mohan Baitha and Ors. v. State of Bihar and Ors. MANU/SC/0217/ 2001; Anju Chaudhary v. State of U.P. and Ors. MANU/SC/1129/2012; State v. Narendra Sah Session Trial No. 8 of 2017

Case Note:

Criminal - Discharge - Jurisdiction - Sections 504, 506 and 376 of the Indian Penal Code, 1860 - Present appeal is directed against the order as passed by the High Court whereby, the High Court declined to interfere with the order as passed by the Sessions Judge, discharging the Accused-Respondent No. 2 of the offence under Section 376 of the IPC on the ground of lack of territorial jurisdiction with liberty to the prosecution to proceed against the Accused in the appropriate Court while also directing transfer of the case in relation to the other offences under Sections 504 and 506 of IPC to the Court of Judicial Magistrate First Class, Gairsain, District Chamoli - Whether learned Sessions Judge, had rightly discharged the Accused-Respondent No. 2 of the offence under Section 376 of IPC for want of territorial jurisdiction?

Facts:

FIR came to be registered and after investigation, a charge-sheet was submitted in the Court of Judicial Magistrate First Class, for offences Under Sections 376, 504 and 506 of IPC; and in view of the involvement of offence under Section 376 of IPC, the case was committed to the Court of Sessions Judge, Chamoli. The order passed by the learned Sessions Judge, Chamoli on the question of framing charge has given rise to the present dispute. The learned Sessions Judge agreed with the contentions so urged on behalf of the Accused and held that the offence Under Section 376 of IPC, which had taken place at Delhi, was not a continuing one; and whatever threat was allegedly given by the Accused to the victim, it did not constitute a kind of offence which could be said to be in the series of same transaction. Therefore, the learned Sessions Judge concluded that the Accused was entitled to be discharged in relation to the offence Under Section 376 of IPC for want of territorial jurisdiction and, in sequel, also found it just and proper to remit the matter to the Court of Judicial Magistrate for trial of the remaining offences pertaining to Sections 504 and 506 of IPC. High Court also declined to interfere with the order as passed by the Sessions Judge, discharging the Accused-Respondent No. 2

Held, while dismissing the appeal

1. Appellant and the Respondent No. 2 were engaged for matrimonial alliance at their village Dangidhar, Tehsil Gairsain, District Chamoli but, the proposal of marriage did not materialise. However, the alleged acts of sexual relationship took place at Delhi in the months of February and March, 2016. The other alleged acts had been of the Respondent No. 2 hurling abuses and extending threats in or around the month of November, 2016, which the Appellant received over telephone at her village. The acts in question were neither proximate in time nor proximate in place; they were not of continuity either. Significantly, while the Appellant had alleged that she submitted to the sexual acts because of the threat by the Respondent No. 2 to snap the proposed alliance but it had not been her case that the Respondent No. 2 attempted to coerce her into the same physical relationship while hurling abuses or threatening to kill at the later part

of time. Thus, it is difficult to find continuity of actions and community of purpose or design in two different acts leading to two different set of offences, i.e., one Under Section 376 of IPC and the other Under Sections 504/506 of IPC. Putting it differently, so far as the act leading to the offence of rape Under Section 376 of IPC is concerned, even as per the allegations of the Appellant, that particular act was a completed one and the original design of subjecting the Appellant to physical relations was accomplished at Delhi In the months of February and March, 2016. There is no allegation of such an activity having continued later or having taken place at Chamoli or even any threat having been extended to the Appellant to again submit to such an activity. Viewed from this angle too, the completed act concerning one offence (Section 376 of IPC) could not have been connected with the other acts leading to other offences. [22.1]

2. Two alleged set of acts, one of sexual exploitation, leading to the offence of rape (Section 376 of IPC) and another of hurling abuses and threats, leading to the offences of insult and intimidation (Sections 504/506 of IPC), are just like chalk and cheese; they cannot be connected together so as to form the same transaction on the facts of this case. [22.2]

3. Offence Under Section 376 of IPC as allegedly committed at Delhi, being different and distinct than the other offences and being not of same transaction, could not have been tried by the Courts at Chamoli. Therefore, the order passed by the learned Sessions Judge calls for no interference. [23]

4. Accused-Respondent No. 2 having gone through the trial in relation to offences Under Sections 504 and 506 of IPC and having been acquitted, cannot be subjected to another trial for the same charges on the same facts. Any such process would be in blatant disregard of the settled principles which disapprove double jeopardy and are precisely contained in Article 20(2) of the Constitution of India as also Section 300 of the Code of Criminal Procedure, 1973. [24.2]

5. On the facts and in the circumstances of this case, the alleged offence under Section 376 of IPC and the other offences under Sections 504 and 506 of IPC do not fall within the ambit of 'one series of acts so connected together as to form the same transaction' for the purpose of trial together in terms of Section 220 of CrPC. Thus, the learned Sessions Judge, had rightly discharged the Accused-Respondent No. 2 of the offence under Section 376 of IPC for want of territorial jurisdiction. [25]

6. Appeal dismissed. [26]

• 28 •

Naresh Kumar Mangla vs. Anita Agarwal and Ors. (17.12.2020 - SC) : MANU/ SC/0951/2020

Relative Section:

Code of Criminal Procedure, 1973 (CrPC) - Section 46(1), Code of Criminal Procedure, 1973 (CrPC) - Section 154, Code of Criminal Procedure, 1973 (CrPC) - Section 438, Code of Criminal Procedure, 1973 (CrPC) - Section 439, Code of Criminal Procedure, 1973 (CrPC) - Section 439(2), Code of Criminal Procedure, 1973 (CrPC) - Section 482; Constitution of India - Article 142, Constitution of India - Article 226; Dowry Prohibition Act, 1961 - Section 3, Dowry Prohibition Act, 1961 - Section 4; Indian Penal Code, 1860 (IPC) - Section 34, Indian Penal Code, 1860 (IPC) - Section 149, Indian Penal Code, 1860 (IPC) - Section 304B, Indian Penal Code, 1860 (IPC) - Section 313, Indian Penal Code, 1860 (IPC) - Section 323, Indian Penal Code, 1860 (IPC) - Section 468, Indian Penal Code, 1860 (IPC) - Section 471, Indian Penal Code, 1860 (IPC) - Section 498A, Indian Penal Code, 1860 (IPC) - Section 506

Hon'bleJudges/Coram:

Dr. D.Y. Chandrachud, Indu Malhotra and Indira Banerjee, JJ.

Equivalent Citation:

2020(12)ADJ622, AIR2021SC277, 2021ALLMR(Cri)3084, 2021(1)BLJ353, 2021CriLJ2066, 2021(1) Crimes 105(SC), I(2021)DMC62SC, 2021(1)HLR271, 2020/INSC/706, 2021(1)JKJ293[SC], 2021(1)MLJ(Crl)170, 2021 (1) MWN (CR.) 109, 2021(1)N.C.C.128,

(2021)15SCC777,   [2020]14SCR294,   2020(Suppl.)Sim.L.C.   401   , 2021(1)UC231

NumberofPagesintheOriginalJudgment: 20

Case Reference:

Puran and Ors. v. Rambilas and Ors. MANU/SC/0326/2001; State and Ors. v. Amarmani Tripathi and Ors. MANU/SC/0677/2005; Jai Prakash Singh v. State of Bihar and Ors. MANU/SC/0224/2012; Neeru Yadav v. State of U.P. and Ors. MANU/SC/1086/2015; Sushila Agarwal v. NCT of Delhi (2020) 5 SCC 1;; State Rep. by the C.B.I. v. Anil Sharma MANU/SC/ 0947/1997; Adri Dharan Das v. State of West Bengal MANU /SC /0120/ 2005; Lavesh v. State (NCT of Delhi) MANU/SC/0701/2012; Siddharam Satlingappa Mhetre v. State of Maharashtra and Ors. MANU/SC/1021/ 2010; D.K. Ganesh Babu v. P.T. Manokaran and Ors. MANU /SC /1086/ 2007; State of Maharashtra and Ors. v. Mohd. Sajid Husain and Ors. MANU/ SC/8008/2007; Union of India (UOI) v. Padam Narain Aggarwal and Ors. MANU/SC/4230/2008; Kanwar Singh Meena v. State of Rajasthan and Ors. MANU/SC/0862/2012; Myakala Dharmarajam and Ors. v. The State of Telangana and Ors. MANU/SC/0010/2020; Pokar Ram v. State of Rajasthan and Ors. MANU/SC/0088/1985; Gurbaksh Singh Sibbia and Ors. v. State of Punjab MANU/SC/0215/1980; Vinay Tyagi v. Irshad Ali and Ors. MANU /SC /1101 /2012; Disha v. State of Gujarat and Ors. MANU/SC/0841/2011; Rubabbuddin Sheikh v. State of Gujarat and Ors. MANU/SC/0024/2010; Pooja Pal v. Union of India (UOI) and Ors. MANU/SC/0071/2016; Dharam Pal v. State of Haryana and Ors. MANU/SC/0118/2016; Arnab Goswami v. Union of India WP (Crl.) 130 of 2020

Case Note:

Criminal - Anticipatory bail - Cancellation of - Sections 304-B, 313, 323, 498-A and 506 of Indian Penal Code, 1860 and Sections 3 and 4 of Dowry Prohibition Act, 1961 - Applications for anticipatory bail filed by four out of five persons who had been named as Accused in case registered under Sections 498A, 304-B, 323, 506 and 313 of Code and Sections 3/4 of Act - Husband of deceased was in custody - Single Judge of High Court allowed applications and granted them anticipatory bail - Hence, present appeal - Whether High Court erred in granting anticipatory bail to accused persons.

Facts:

FIR was registered against accused persons for offence under Sections 498A, 304-B, 323, 506 and 313 of the Indian Penal Code and Sections 3/4 of the Dowry Prohibition Act, 1961. The Sessions Judge noted that besides naming the Accused specifically, there were also allegations against the four Respondents in the FIR of torturing the deceased and of making demands for dowry. Non-bailable warrants were issued against the four Accused. Applications for anticipatory bail were filed on their behalf before the High Court. A Single Judge of the High Court allowed the applications and granted them anticipatory bail.

Held, while allowing the appeal:

(i) The judgment of the Single Judge of the High Court was unsustainable. The FIR contains a recital of allegations bearing on the role of the Accused in demanding dowry, of the prior incidents of assault and the payment of moneys by cheque to the in-laws of the deceased. The FIR had referred to the telephone calls which were received both from the father-in-law of the deceased on the morning and from the deceased on two occasions on the same day-a few hours before her body was found. The grant of anticipatory bail in such a serious offence would operate to obstruct the investigation. The FIR by a father who had suffered the death of his daughter in these circumstances could not be regarded as engineered to falsely implicate the spouse of the deceased and his family. [19]

(ii) It was necessary to entrust a further investigation of the case to the CBI in exercise of the powers of this Court under Article 142 of the Constitution. The conduct of the investigating authorities from the stage of arriving at the scene of occurrence to the filing of the charge-sheet did not inspire confidence in the robustness of the process. A perusal of the charge-sheet evinces a perfunctory rendition of the investigating authorities duty by a bare reference to the facts and the presumption under Section 304B of the IBC (slc Indian Penal Code) when the death occurs within seven years of the marriage. The stance taken by the Deputy Superintendent of Police in the Counter Affidavit, filed a few days after forwarding the charge-sheet, travels beyond the scope of the investigation recorded in the charge-sheet with respect to the veracity of the suicide note, medical examination of injuries and the past miscarriages of the deceased. Critical facts of the money trail between the deceased, her father (the informant), and the Accused and the call history of A2, the informant and the deceased were unexplored. No attempt at custodial interrogation of the applicants was made between the issuance of non-bailable warrants and interim protection from arrest by the High Court granted. Upon questioning during the hearing, the Counsel for the State answered that no investigation on the allegation of murder had been conducted. It would indeed be a travesty if this Court were to ignore the glaring deficiencies in the investigation conducted so far, irrespective of the stage of the proceedings or the nature of the question before this Court. The status of the Accused as propertied and wealthy persons of influence in Agra and the conduct of the investigation thus far diminishes this Court's faith in directing a further investigation by the same authorities. The cause of justice would not be served if the Court were to confine the scope of its examination to the wisdom of granting anticipatory bail and ignore the possibility of a trial being concluded on the basis of a deficient investigation at best or a biased one at worst. [23]

Disposition: Appeal Allowed

Nallapareddy Sridhar Reddy vs. The State of Andhra Pradesh and Ors. (21.01.2020 - SC) : MANU/SC/0057/ 2020

Relative Section:

Code of Criminal Procedure, 1973 (CrPC) - Section 161, Code of Criminal Procedure, 1973 (CrPC) - Section 216, Code of Criminal Procedure, 1973 (CrPC) - Section 216(1), Code of Criminal Procedure, 1973 (CrPC) - Section 216(2), Code of Criminal Procedure, 1973 (CrPC) - Section 216(3), Code of Criminal Procedure, 1973 (CrPC) Section 216(4), Code of Criminal Procedure, 1973 (CrPC) - Section 216(5), Code of Criminal Procedure, 1973 (CrPC) - Section 217; Constitution of India - Article 136; Dowry Prohibition Act, 1961 - Section 3, Dowry Prohibition Act, 1961 - Section 4; Explosives Act, 1884; Indian Penal Code, 1860 (IPC) - Section 302, Indian Penal Code, 1860 (IPC) - Section 304B, Indian Penal Code, 1860 (IPC) - Section 323, Indian Penal Code, 1860 (IPC) - Section 376, Indian Penal Code, 1860 (IPC) - Section 406, Indian Penal Code, 1860 (IPC) - Section 417, Indian Penal Code, 1860 (IPC) - Section 420, Indian Penal Code, 1860 (IPC) - Section 498A; Terrorist and Disruptive Activities (Prevention) Act, 1987

Hon'bleJudges/Coram:

Dr. D.Y. Chandrachud and Hrishikesh Roy, JJ

Equivalent Citation:

2020(211)AIC191, 2020(211)AIC191, AIR2020SC753, 2020 (1) ALD(Crl.) 759 (SC), 2020 (112) ACC 850, 2020 (2) ALT (Crl.) 17 (A.P.), 2020CriLJ1792, 2020(1)Crimes198(SC), 2020(1)CriminalCC787, 2020 (1) CT C810,2020/INSC/68, 2020(1)J.L.J.R.363, 2020(1)JKJ219[SC], 2020-2-LW(Crl)326, 2020(1)PLJR407, 2020 (1) RCR(Criminal)787, (2020)12SCC467, 2020 (3) SCJ 667, [2020]1SCR1116, 2020(1)UC30

NumberofPagesintheOriginalJudgment:11

Case Reference:

Onkar Nath Mishra and Ors. v. State (NCT of Delhi) and Anr. MANU/SC/0134/2008; Hridaya Ranjan Pd. Verma & Ors. v. State of Bihar and Another MANU/SC/0223/2000; Anant Prakash Sinha v. State of Haryana and Ors. MANU/SC/0279/2016; Sajjan Kumar v. Central Bureau of Investigation MANU/SC/0741/2010; P. Kartikalakshmi v. Ganesh and Ors. MANU/SC/1321/2014; C.B.I. v. Karimullah Osan Khan MANU /SC/ 0167 /2014; Jasvinder Saini and Ors. v. State (Govt. of NCT of Delhi) MANU/ SC/0642/2013

Case Note:

Criminal - Additional charges - Framing of - Section 216 of Code of Criminal Procedure, 1973 and Sections 406 and 420 of Indian Penal Code, 1860 - First Information Report was lodged by fourth Respondent, alleging that Appellant and members of his family had harassed his daughter with demands for money and transfer of land in their names - Trial Court framed charges against Appellant only for offences under Section 498A of Indian Penal Code, 1860 along with Sections 3 and 4 of Dowry Prohibition Act 1961 - Application was filed by Public Prosecutor under Section 216 of Code for framing of additional charges - Trial Court concluded that ingredients for offences under Sections 406 and 420 of Code were not made out and rejected application for framing additional charges - Fourth Respondent filed revision petition before High Court against order of Trial Court - Single Judge of High Court set aside Trial Court's order by holding that Trial Court while rejecting application under Section 216 did not disclose reasons - Hence, present appeal - Whether High Court was right in adding charges under Sections 406 and 420 of Code.

Facts:

A First Information Report was lodged by the fourth Respondent, who was the father-in-law of the Appellant, alleging that the Appellant and the members of his family had harassed his daughter with demands for money and transfer of land in their names. A charge-sheet was filed against the Appellant and his parents for offences under Section 498A of the Indian Penal Code along with Sections 3 and 4 of the Dowry Prohibition Act 1961. An additional charge-sheet had been filed by the investigating officer implicating the Appellant for crimes under Sections 406 and 420, charges were not framed by the trial judge under those provisions. The Trial Court framed charges against the Appellant only for offences mentioned in the original charge-sheet under Section 498A of Code along with Sections 3 and 4 of the Dowry Prohibition Act. An application was filed by the Public Prosecutor under Section 216 of Code of Criminal Procedure for alteration of charge. The Trial Court after hearing arguments on behalf of both the sides and perusing the material available on record concluded that the ingredients for offences under Sections 406 and 420 Indian Penal Code were not made out and rejected the application for framing additional charges. The fourth Respondent filed a revision petition before the High Court against the above order of the Trial Court. A Single Judge of the High Court allowed the revision petition and set aside the Trial Court's order. The High Court held that the Trial Court while rejecting the application under Section 216 did not disclose the reasons for concluding that the ingredients of Sections 406 and 420 were not attracted and only touched upon the lapses of the prosecution in not seeking an alteration of charges during the course of the trial.

Held, while dismissing the appeal:

(i) The test adopted by the High Court was correct and in accordance with decisions of this Court. In the counter affidavit filed by the fourth Respondent before this Court, depositions of witnesses and their cross-examination had been annexed. The material on record supports the possibility that the Appellant demanded certain amount from complainant, in order to secure a doctor's job for the complainant's daughter in the foreign country. According to complainant, he borrowed the amount and paid it to the Appellant. Without pronouncing on the probative value of such evidence, there exists sufficient material on record that shows a connection or link with the ingredients of the offences under Sections 406 and 420 of the Indian Penal Code, and the charges sought to be added. [23]

(ii) The veracity of the depositions made by the witnesses was a question of trial and need not be determined at the time of framing of charge. Appreciation of evidence on merit was to be done by the court only after the charges had been framed and the trial had commenced.

However, for the purpose of framing of charge the court needs to prima facie determine that there exists sufficient material for the commencement of trial. The High Court had relied upon the materials on record and concluded that the ingredients of the offences under Sections 406 and 420 of the Indian Penal Code were attracted. The High Court had spelt out the reasons that had necessitated the addition of the charge and hence, the impugned order did not warrant any interference. [24]

Ratio Decidendi: The test to be adopted by the court while deciding upon an addition or alteration of a charge is that the material brought on record needs to have a direct link or nexus with the ingredients of the alleged offence.

Disposition: In Favour of State

CHAPTER ELEVEN

Sonu vs. Sonu Yadav and Ors. (05.04.20– SC) : MANU 21 /SC/0243/2021

Relative Section:

Code of Criminal Procedure, 1973 (CrPC) - Section 439; Dowry Prohibition Act, 1961 - Section 3, Dowry Prohibition Act, 1961 - Section 4; Evidence Act - Section 113A, Evidence Act - Section 113B; Indian Penal Code, 1860 (IPC) - Section 304B, Indian Penal Code, 1860 (IPC) - Section 498A

Hon'bleJudges/Coram:

Dr. D.Y. Chandrachud and M.R. Shah, JJ.

Equivalent Citation:

2022(1)ACR740, 2021(5)ADJ156, 2021(222)AIC166, AIR2021SC1950, 2021 (2) ALD(Crl.) 228 (SC), 2021 (116) ACC 650, 2021ALLMR(Cri)2667, 2021(2)BomCR(Cri)695, 2021CriLJ2464, 2021(2)CriminalCC604, (2021)4GLR2931, 2021/INSC/225, 2021(2)JKJ414[SC], 2021(2)RCR(Criminal)650, 2021(3)RLW2379(SC), (2021)15SCC228, [2021]7SCR78, 2021(3)UC1396

NumberofPagesintheOriginalJudgment: 6

Case Reference:

Brij Nandan Jaiswal v. Munna and Ors. MANU/SC/8441/2008

Case Note:

Criminal - Bail - Cancellation of - Sections 304B and 498A of Indian Penal Code, 1860 and Sections 3 and 4 of - First Information Report was registered for offences under Sections 498A and 304-B of Code and Sections 3 and 4 of Act and charge-sheet had been submitted - Bail application filed by first Respondent was rejected by Sessions Judge - High Court was thereafter allowed bail application - Hence, present appeal - Whether High Court erred in grating bail to Respondents.

Facts:

A First Information Report was registered for offences under Sections 498A and 304-B of the Indian Penal Code and Sections 3 and 4 of the Dowry Prohibition Act 1861. A charge-sheet had been submitted for offences alleged under Sections 498-A and 304-B of the Indian Penal Code and Sections 3 and 4 of the Dowry Prohibition Act. The bail application filed by the first Respondent was rejected by the Sessions Judge. The High Court was thereafter moved in a bail application allowed the application.

Held, while allowing the appeal:

(i) It was not in dispute that the first Respondent was married to the sister of the Appellant. She died within a year of the marriage. There were specific allegations in the First Information Report in regard to the demand of dowry, as well as in regard to a phone call being received from the Accused in close proximity to the death of the sister of the Appellant when a demand for additional amounts of money was made. The submission in support of bail recorded by the High Court was that the sister of the Appellant was undergoing treatment for a mental illness. In this context, it was material to note that in the bail application, the plea was that the deceased was suffering from severe headache and was mentally disturbed since the past nine months and that she was taken to a doctor by the first Respondent. A copy of the medical prescription, which had been submitted before this Court, would prima facie indicate that there was no serious ailment. The medical prescription of the Ayurvedic doctor and the remedies prescribed belie such a claim. Prima facie, there are serious allegations in the FIR in regard to the harassment suffered by the deceased in close proximity to her death over demands for dowry by the Accused. In view of the provisions of Section 304-B of the Indian Penal Code, as well as the presumption which arises under Section 113-B of the Evidence Act, the High Court was clearly not justified in granting bail. [9]

(ii) In the earlier part of this judgment, this court had extracted the lone sentence in the order of the High Court which is intended to display some semblance of reasoning for justifying the grant of bail. The sentence which we have extracted earlier contains an omnibus amalgam of the entire facts and circumstances of the case, submissions of Counsel for the parties, the nature of offence, evidence and complicity of Accused. This was followed by an observation that the applicant has made out a case for bail, without expressing any opinion on the merits of the case. This did not constitute the kind of reasoning which was expected of a judicial order. The High Court could not be oblivious, in a case such as the present, of the seriousness of the alleged offence, where a woman had met an unnatural end within a year of marriage. The seriousness of the alleged offence had to be evaluated in the backdrop of the allegation that she was being harassed for dowry and that a telephone call was received from the Accused in close-proximity to the time of death, making a demand. There were specific allegations of harassment against the Accused on the ground of dowry. An order without reasons was fundamentally contrary to the norms which guide the judicial process. The administration of criminal justice by the High Court could not be reduced to a mantra containing a recitation of general observations. That there had been a judicious application of mind by the judge who is deciding an application under Section 439 of the Code of Criminal Procedure must emerge from the quality of the reasoning which was embodied in the order granting bail. While the reasons may be brief, it was the quality of the reasons which matters the most. That was because the reasons in a judicial order unravel the thought process of a trained judicial mind. The reasons indicated in the judgment of the High Court in this case were becoming increasingly familiar in matters which come to this Court. It was time that such a practice was discontinued and that the reasons in support of orders granting bail comport with a judicial process which brings credibility to the administration of criminal justice. [11]

(iii) Therefore, set aside the impugned judgment and order of the Single Judge of the High Court granting bail to the first Respondent. [13]

Disposition: Appeal Allowed

Nathu Singh and Ors. vs. State of Uttar Pradesh and Ors. (28.05.2021 - SC) : MANU/SC/0360/2021

Relative Section:

Code of Criminal Procedure, 1973 (CrPC) - Section 437(3), Code of Criminal Procedure, 1973 (CrPC) - Section 438, Code of Criminal Procedure, 1973 (CrPC) - Section 438(1), Code of Criminal Procedure, 1973 (CrPC) - Section 438(2), Code of Criminal Procedure, 1973 (CrPC) - Section 438(3), Code of Criminal Procedure, 1973 (CrPC) - Section 482; Dowry Prohibition Act, 1961 - Section 3, Dowry Prohibition Act, 1961 - Section 4; Indian Penal Code, 1860 (IPC) - Section 34, Indian Penal Code, 1860 (IPC) - Section 304B, Indian Penal Code, 1860 (IPC) - Section 307, Indian Penal Code, 1860 (IPC) - Section 498A, Indian Penal Code, 1860 (IPC) - Section 504

Hon'bleJudges/Coram:

N.V. Ramana, C.J.I., Surya Kant and Aniruddha Bose, JJ.

Equivalent Citation:

2021(6)ADJ268, 2021(223)AIC117, AIR2021SC2606, AIR2021SC2606, 2021 (2) ALD(Crl.) 299 (SC), 2021 (117) ACC 339, 2021ALLMR(Cri)2686, 2021ALLMR(Cri)2686, 2021 (2) ALT (Crl.) 259 (A.P.), 2021 (4) BL J98,2021 CriLJ 2593, 2021CriLJ2593, 2021(2)Crimes427(SC), 2021(3)CriminalCC468, 2021/INSC/300, 2021 (2)J.L.J.R.415, 2021 (3) JKJ168[SC], 2021 (4) KHC 173, 2021(3)MLJ(Crl)119, 2021 (2) MWN (CR.) 427, 2021(2)N.C.C.552, 2021 (2)PLJR423, (2021)203PLR108,

(2021)3PLR108, 2021(3)RCR(Criminal)162, (2021) 6SCC64, [2021]6SCR599, 2021 (3)UC1456 I

NumberofPagesintheOriginalJudgment: 8

Case Reference:

P. Chidambaram v. Directorate of Enforcement MANU/SC/1209/2019; Lal Kamlendra Pratap Singh v. State of U.P. and Ors. MANU/SC/0449/ 2009; M. Siddiq (D) thr. L.Rs. v. Mahant Suresh Das and Ors. MANU/SC/ 1538/2019; Gurbaksh Singh Sibbia and Ors. v. State of Punjab MANU/SC/ 0215/1980; Amrawati and Anr. v. State of U.P. MANU/UP/0819/2004 : 2004 (57) ALR 290

Case Note:

Criminal - Anticipatory Bail - FIR registered under Sections 304B and 498A of the Indian Penal Code, 1860 (IPC) read with Sections 3 and 4 of the Dowry Prohibition Act - In other appeal FIR registered under Sections 307, 504 and 34 of the IPC - High Court vide impugned declined plea of anticipatory bail - However, protection from coercive action granted for 90 days - Whether High Court, while dismissing the anticipatory bail applications of the Respondents, could have granted them protection from arrest?

Facts:

Appellant's daughter was married to R2. She died under suspicious circumstances in her matrimonial home. FIR was registered under Sections 304B and 498A, Indian Penal Code by the Respondents due to a dispute between the parties relating to encroachment read with Sections 3 and 4 of the Dowry Prohibition Act against R2 to 5.In the second case, the allegations were that Appellant's brother and the latter's two sons were attacked of land. The two sons were attacked on their vital parts, with one of them suffering a skull fracture as a result of which he was in a coma for one week. The other had lacerations on his head. The complainant registered FIR under Sections 307, 504 and 34, Indian Penal Code. High Court vide impugned orderswhile dismissing anticipatory bail application of the Respondents-Accused, granted them 90 days to surrender before the Trial Court to seek regular bail. Protection from coercive action for the said period however was granted. Hence, the present appeal.

Held, while allowing the Appeals:

Discretionary power cannot be exercised in an untrammeled manner. The Court must take into account the statutory scheme under Section 438, Code of Criminal Procedure, particularly, the proviso to Section 438(1),

Code of Criminal Procedure, and balance the concerns of the investigating agency, complainant and the society at large with the concerns/interest of the applicant. [25]

Impugned orders does not meet any of the standards as laid down. High Court granted impugned relief without assigning any reasons. [26]

Impugned orders does not withstand legal scrutiny. The resultant effect of the High Court's orders was that neither Respondents found entitled to pre-arrest bail, nor could they be arrested for a long duration. [27]

Appeals allowed. The impugned order of the High Court to the extent of granting protection for 90 days to the Respondents-Accused are set aside, leaving it open to the Investigating Agency to proceed in the matters in accordance with law.[28]

Disposition: In Favour of Accused

Parvez Noordin Lokhandwalla vs. State of Maharashtra and Ors. (01.10.2020 - SC) : MANU/SC/0743/2020

Relative Section:

Code of Criminal Procedure, 1973 (CrPC) - Section 156(3), Code of Criminal Procedure, 1973 (CrPC) - Section 340, Code of Criminal Procedure, 1973 (CrPC) - Section 437(3), Code of Criminal Procedure, 1973 (CrPC) - Section 438, Code of Criminal Procedure, 1973 (CrPC) - Section 438(1), Code of Criminal Procedure, 1973 (CrPC) - Section 438(2), Code of Criminal Procedure, 1973 (CrPC) - Section 439, Code of Criminal Procedure, 1973 (CrPC) - Section 439(1); Dowry Prohibition Act, 1961 - Section 3, Dowry Prohibition Act, 1961 - Section 4; Indian Penal Code, 1860 (IPC) - Section 34, Indian Penal Code, 1860 (IPC) - Section 323, Indian Penal Code, 1860 (IPC) - Section 341, Indian Penal Code, 1860 (IPC) - Section 379, Indian Penal Code, 1860 (IPC) - Section 420, Indian Penal Code, 1860 (IPC) - Section 467, Indian Penal Code, 1860 (IPC) - Section 468, Indian Penal Code, 1860 (IPC) - Section 469, Indian Penal Code, 1860 (IPC) - Section 470, Indian Penal Code, 1860 (IPC) - Section 471, Indian Penal Code, 1860 (IPC) - Section 474, Indian Penal Code, 1860 (IPC) - Section 498A, Indian Penal Code, 1860 (IPC) - Section 506; United States Immigration and Nationality Act 1952 - Section 1182(a), United States Immigration and Nationality Act 1952 - Section 1182(h), United States Immigration and Nationality Act 1952 - Section 1229b(a)

Hon'bleJudges/Coram:

Dr. D.Y. Chandrachud and Indira Banerjee, JJ.

Equivalent **Citation**: 2021(217)AIC207,AIR2021SC641,2020ALLMR(Cri)3708, 2020 (3) ALT (Crl.) 334 (A.P.),2022CriLJ1172,2021(2)Crimes71(SC),2021(1)CriminalCC1,2020/INSC/573,2020(4)MLJ(Crl)327,2020 (4)RCR(Criminal)649, (2020)10SCC77, 2020 (9-10) SCJ 702,[2020]11SCR117, 2020(3)UC1764

NumberofPagesintheOriginalJudgment:15

Case Reference:

Kunal Kumar Tiwari v. The State of Bihar and Ors. MANU/SC/1325/2017; Dataram Singh v. State of Uttar Pradesh and Ors. MANU/SC/0085/2018; Sumit Mehta v. State of N.C.T. of Delhi MANU/SC/0935/2013; Lokhandwala Weigh Bridge v. Asam Transport RCS/200577/2005; Firdaus Rajabali Merchant v. Farida Firoz Lokhandwala RCC/420380/2010; Firdaus Rajabali Merchant v. Parvez Noor Lokhandwala CR. MA/300998/2013; Firoz Pirbhai Lokhandwala v. Nooruddin Pirbhai Lokhandwala RCS/201541/2001; Mehraj Rajabali Merchant v. Parvez Noor Lokhandwala and Ors. Civil MA/286/2019; Parvez Noor Lokhandwala v. Firdaus Rajabali Merchant RCS/200143/2011; Shalin Noor Lokhandwala v. Hindustan Petroleum Civil MA/100012/2008; Farida Noor Lokhandwala v. Farida Firoz Lokhandwala RCS/201901/2012; Farida Noor Lokhandwala v. Farida Firoz Lokhandwala Sp. Case/200905/2012; Firdaus Rajabali Merchant v. Farida Firoz Lokhandwala Sp. Case/200393/2010; Firdaus Rajabali Merchant v. Parvez N. Lokhandwala Misc. Cr. Application 799/2017; Mehraj Rajabali Merchant v. Parvez Noor Lokhandwala and Ors. MCA/10/2020; Mehraj Rajabali Merchant v. Parvez Noor Lokhandwala and Ors. MA/200687/2015; Farida Firoz Lokhandwala v. Farida Noor Lokhandwala Civil MA/200404/2015; Mehraj Rajabali Merchant v. Parvez Nooruddin Lokhandwala RCS/200566/2013; Mehraj Rajabali Merchant v. Parvez Noor Lokhandwala Sp. Case/424/2017; Farida Noor Lokhandwala v. Farida Firoz Lokhandwala MA/200315/2015; Farida N. Lokhandwalla v. Firdaus Rajabali Merchant and Ors. M.A./91/2014; Parvez N. Lokhandwalla v. State of Maharashtra SLP (CRL) Nos. 3420 and 3034/2020; Parvez N. Lokhandwalla v. State of Maharashtra LD/VC/BA/24/2020; Parvez N. Lokhandwalla v. State of Maharashtra and Ors. ASDB-LD-VC No. 102 of 2020 and WP/891/2018; Barun Chandra Thakur v. Ryan Augustine Pinto Criminal Appeal No. 1618 of 2019 (Arising out of SLP (Crl.) No. 9873 of 2019); Ganpati Ramnath v. State of Bihar Crlmp. Nos. 6304 & 6305/2017;

K. Mohammed v. The State of Kerala Criminal Appeal No. 547/2012; Tarun Trikha v. State of West Bengal Special Leave to Appeal Crl. No. 4643/2015; Pitam Pradhan v. State of A.P. Special Leave to Appeal (Crl) No. 9664/2013

Case Note:

Criminal - Travel Permission - Pendency of First Information Report (FIR) under Sections 420, 467, 468, 469, 470, 471 and 474 read with Section 34 of the Indian Penal Code 1860 (IPC) - Enlarged on Bail subject to conditions - Appellant an Indian citizen, holding Indian passport and a Green Cardto reside in US - Permission sought to validate Green Card as per US Immigration and Nationality Act 1952 - High Court declined to relax bail conditions - Whether Appellant entitled to get permission to travel during the pendency of FIR by relaxing bail conditions?

Facts:

Appellant, an Indian citizen and holder of Indian Passport was also holding US Green Card. He, vide private complaint, was alleged of fabricating a Power of Attorney by forging the signature of his brother. Investigation under Section 156(3) of the Code of Criminal Procedure 1973 was directed. An FIR was registered against the Appellant alleging offences punishable under Sections 420, 467, 468, 469, 470, 471 and 474 of the Indian Penal Code 1860read with Section 34. He was arrested and then enlarged on temporary bail subject to conditions. He sought the leave of High Court to travel abroad (USA) on the premise that being a Green Card holder, it was mandatory for him to return to the US within a stipulated period of his departure from that country. Failure to travel could devoid revalidation of the Green Card. The High Court declined to relax the conditions imposed by it for the grant of interim bail on the ground that an FIR was against the Appellant. Hence, the present appeal.

IIeld, while disposing the Appeal:

i. Though the competent court is empowered to exercise its discretion to impose "any condition" for the grant of bail Under Sections 437(3) and 439(1)(a) of the Code of Criminal Procedure, the discretion of the court has to be guided by the need to facilitate the administration of justice, secure the presence of the Accused and ensure that the liberty of the Accused is not misused to impede the investigation, overawe the witnesses or obstruct the course of justice. Several decisions of this Court have dwelt on the nature of the conditions which can legitimately be imposed both in the context of bail and anticipatory bail. [14]

ii. In evaluating the issue, regard must be to the nature of the allegations, the conduct of the Appellant and above all, the need to ensure that he does not pose a risk of evading the prosecution. The details which have been furnished to the Court by the Appellant, indicate that he has regularly travelled between the US and India on as many as sixteen occasions between 2015 and 2020. He has maintained a close contact with India. The view of the High Court that he has no contact with India is contrary to the material on record. The lodging of an FIR should not in the facts of the present case be a bar on the travel of the Appellant to the US for eight weeks to attend to the business of revalidating his Green Card. The conditions which a court imposes for the grant of bail - in this case temporary bail - have to balance the public interest in the enforcement of criminal justice with the rights of the Accused. The human right to dignity and the protection of constitutional safeguards should not become illusory by the imposition of conditions which are disproportionate to the need to secure the presence of the Accused, the proper course of investigation and eventually to ensure a fair trial. The conditions which are imposed by the court must bear a proportional relationship to the purpose of imposing the conditions. The nature of the risk which is posed by the grant of permission as sought in this case must be carefully evaluated in each case. [21]

iii. The Appellant is an Indian citizen and holds an Indian passport. While it is true that an FIR has been lodged against the Appellant, that should not in itself prevent him from travelling to the US, where he is a resident since 1985, particularly when it has been drawn to the attention of the High Court and this Court that serious consequences would ensue in terms of the invalidation of the Green Card if the Appellant were not permitted to travel. The record indicates the large amount of litigation between the family of the Appellant and the complainant. Notwithstanding or perhaps because of this, the Appellant has frequently travelled between the US and India even after the filing of the complaint and the FIR. The application for modification was incorrectly rejected by the High Court and the Appellant ought to have been allowed to travel to the US for a period of eight weeks. Appellant accordingly permitted to do so, subject to his furnishing an undertaking to this Court before the date of travel that he will return to India after the expiry of a period of eight weeks and that he shall be available on all dates of hearing before the court of criminal jurisdiction, unless specifically exempted from personal appearance. The undertaking shall be filed in this Court before the Appellant undertakes travel. On the return of the Appellant after eight weeks and if it becomes necessary for him to travel to the US, the Appellant shall apply to the concerned court for permission to travel and any such application shall be considered on its own merits by the competent court. The Appellant shall travel only upon the grant of permission and subject to the terms imposed. The passport of the Appellant shall be handed over to the Appellant to facilitate his travel, subject to the condition that he shall deposit it with the investigating officer immediately on his return. [24]

Disposition: Disposed of

Preet Pal Singh vs. The State of Uttar Pradesh and Ors. (14.08.2020 – SC) : MANU/ SC/0591/2020

Relative Section:

Code of Criminal Procedure, 1973 (CrPC) - Section 313, Code of Criminal Procedure, 1973 (CrPC) - Section 389, Code of Criminal Procedure, 1973 (CrPC) - Section 389(1), Code of Criminal Procedure, 1973 (CrPC) - Section 389(3), Code of Criminal Procedure, 1973 (CrPC) - Section 439; Dowry Prohibition (Amendment) Act, 1986; Dowry Prohibition Act, 1961 - Section 3, Dowry Prohibition Act, 1961 - Section 4; Indian Penal Code, 1860 (IPC) - Section 304B, Indian Penal Code, 1860 (IPC) - Section 406, Indian Penal Code, 1860 (IPC) - Section 411, Indian Penal Code, 1860 (IPC) - Section 498A

Hon'bleJudges/Coram:

Arun Mishra and Indira Banerjee, JJ.

EquivalentCitation:2020(3)ACR2128,2021(2)ACR2012, 2020(8)ADJ612,2020(214)AIC129,AIR2020 SC3995,2020(2)ALD(Crl.)707(SC),2020(113)ACC679, 2020(5)BLJ355,2020(3)Crimes147(SC),2021(3) Criminal CC78, I(2021)DMC45SC, 2021(3)HLR792, 2020/INSC/493, 2020(3)J.L.J.R.421, 2020(4) JKJ123 [SC],2020(3)MLJ(Crl)633,2020(3)PLJR371, 2020(4)RCR(Criminal)848,(2020)8SCC645, [2020]6SCR967, 2020 (2)UC1281

NumberofPagesintheOriginalJudgment: 9

Case Reference:

Kashmira Singh v. The State of Punjab MANU/SC/0099/1977; Babu Singh and Ors. v. State of U.P. MANU/SC/0059/1978; The State of Punjab v. Iqbal Singh and Ors. MANU /SC/0354/1991; Kalyan Chandra Sarkar v. Rajesh Ranjan and Ors. MANU /SC/0214/2004; Chaman Lal v. State of U.P. and Ors. MANU/SC/0631/2004; Mauji Ram v. State of Uttar Pradesh and Ors. MANU/SC/0991/2019; Lokesh Singh v. State of U.P. and Ors. MANU/SC/8138/2008; Dataram Singh v. State of Uttar Pradesh and Ors. MANU/SC/0085/2018; Vinod Singh Negi v. The State of Uttar Pradesh and Ors. MANU/SC/1093/2019; Ajay Kumar Sharma v. State of U.P. and Ors. (2005) 7 SCC 507

Case Note:

Criminal - Suspension of sentence - Validity of - Sections 304B, 406 and 498A of Indian Penal Code, 1860, Section 389 of Code of Criminal Procedure, 1973 and Sections 3 and 4 of Dowry Prohibition Act, 1961 - Sessions Court convicted Respondent No.2 for offences under Sections 304B, 498A and 406 of Code and Sections 3 and 4 of Act - Being aggrieved by conviction and sentence, Respondent No. 2 filed appeal in High Court - After filing appeal, Respondent No. 2 filed application inter alia praying that he be enlarged on bail, during pendency of appeal - High Court granted bail to Respondent No. 2 by staying execution of sentences of imprisonment - Hence, present appeal - Whether High Court erred in granting bail to Respondent No. 2 by staying execution of sentences of imprisonment.

Facts:

The Sessions Court convicted Respondent No. 2 for offences under Sections 304B, 498A and 406 of the Indian Penal Code (IPC) and Sections 3 and 4 of the Dowry Prohibition Act, 1961 by staying execution of the sentences of imprisonment. Being aggrieved by the conviction and sentence, the Respondent No. 2 filed an appeal in the High Court. After filing the appeal, the Respondent No. 2 filed application inter alia praying that he be enlarged on bail, during the pendency of the aforesaid appeal. The said application had been allowed. The High Court granted bail to the Respondent No. 2, husband of the deceased victim, convicted by a judgment of the Additional District and Sessions Judge/Special Judge (EC Act), for offences under Sections 304B, 498A and 406 of the Indian Penal Code (IPC) and Sections 3 and 4 of the Dowry Prohibition Act, 1961 by staying execution of the sentences of imprisonment.

Held, while allowing the appeal:

(i) It was nobody's case that the death of the victim was accidental or natural. There was evidence of demand of dowry, which the Trial Court had considered. The death took place within seven or eight months and there was oral evidence of the parents of cruelty and torture immediately preceding the death. There was also evidence of payment to the Respondent-Accused by the victim's brother. The Respondent No. 2 had not been able to demonstrate any apparent and/or obvious illegality or error in the judgment of the Sessions Court, to call for suspension of execution of the sentence. [38]

(ii) In considering an application for suspension of sentence, the Appellate Court was only to examine if there was such patent infirmity in the order of conviction that renders the order of conviction prima facie erroneous. Where there was evidence that had been considered by the Trial Court, it was not open to a Court considering application under Section 389 to re-assess and/or re-analyze the same evidence and take a different view, to suspend the execution of the sentence and release the convict on bail. [39]

(iii) It was difficult to appreciate how the High Court could casually have suspended the execution of the sentence and granted bail to the Respondent No. 2 without recording any reasons, with the casual observation of force in the argument made on behalf of the Appellant before the High Court, that was, the Respondent No. 2. In effect, at the stage of an application under Section 389 of the Code of Criminal Procedure, the High Court found merit in the submission that the brother of the victim not having been examined, the contention of the Respondent No. 2, being the Appellant before the High Court, that the amount was taken as a loan was not refuted, ignoring the evidence relied upon by the Sessions Court, including the oral evidence of the victim's parents. [41]

(iv) From the evidence of the Prosecution witnesses, it transpires that the Appellant had spent money beyond his financial capacity, at the wedding of the victim and had even gifted an car. The hapless parents were hoping against hope that there would be an amicable settlement. Even as late the brother of the victim paid amount to the Respondent No. 2. The failure to lodge an FIR complaining of dowry and harassment before the death of the victim, was inconsequential. The parents and other family members of the victim obviously would not want to precipitate a complete breakdown of the marriage by lodging an FIR against the Respondent No. 2

and his parents, while the victim was alive. [42]

(v) The impugned order of the High Court was set aside and the Respondent No. 2 was directed to surrender for being taken into custody. [43]

Disposition: In Favour of Accused

Charan Singh vs. The State of Uttarakhand (20.04.2023 - SC) : MANU/SC/0421/2023

Relative Section:

Dowry Prohibition Act, 1961 - Section 2; Indian Evidence Act, 1872 - Section 113B; Indian Penal Code, 1860 (IPC) - Section 201, Indian Penal Code, 1860 (IPC) - Section 304B, Section 498A

Hon'bleJudges/Coram:

Abhay Shreeniwas Oka and Rajesh Bindal, JJ.

Equivalent Citation: AIR2023SC2095, 2023ALLMR(Cri)2698, 2023(2)CriminalCC59, II(2023) DMC 466SC , 2023(2)HLR218, 2023/INSC/404

NumberofPagesintheOriginalJudgment: 9

Case Reference:

Baijnath and Ors.v.State of Madhya Pradesh MANU/SC/1501/2016; Shindo and Ors. v. State of Punjab MANU /SC/0499/2011; Rajeev Kumar v. State of Haryana MANU/SC/1144/2013; K. Prema S. Rao and Ors. v. Yadla Srinivasa Rao and Ors. MANU/SC/0890/2002

Case Note:

Criminal - Acquittal - Dowry death - Sections 201, 304B and 498A of Indian Penal Code, 1860 and Section 113B of Indian Evidence Act, 1872 - FIR was registered against accused persons for offence of dowry death, cruelty and destruction of evidence punishable under Sections 304B, 498A and 201 of Code - Matter was investigated and charge sheet was filed against accused persons - Trial Court, after evaluating evidence, convicted Appellant and other accused person under Sections 304B, 498A and 201 of Code - In appeal filed by convicts before High Court, conviction and sentence of brother-in-law and mother-in-lawwere set aside and they were acquitted of charges, whereas conviction of Appellant was upheld - Hence, present appeal - Whether prosecution prove its case beyond reasonable doubt.

Facts:

An FIR was registered against accused persons for offence of dowry death, cruelty and destruction of evidence punishable under Sections 304B, 498A and 201 of Code. The matter was investigated and chargesheet was filed against accused persons. The prosecution examined six witnesses and defence examined one witness. The Trial Court, after evaluating the evidence, convicted Appellant and other accused under Sections 304B, 498A and 201 of Code. In appeal filed by the convicts before the High Court, the conviction and sentence of brother-in-law and mother-in-law under Section 304B, 498A and 201 Indian Penal Code were set aside and they were acquitted of the charges, whereas the conviction of the Appellant was upheld.

Held, while allowing the appeal:

(i) In the evidence led by the prosecution, none of the witnesses stated about the cruelty or harassment to the deceased by the Appellant or any of his family members on account of demand of dowry soon before the death or otherwise. Rather harassment had not been narrated by anyone. It was only certain oral averments regarding demand of motorcycle and land which was also much prior to the incident. The said evidence led by the prosecution did not fulfil the pre-requisites to invoke presumption under Section 304B Indian Penal Code or Section 113B of the Indian Evidence Act. Even the ingredients of Section 498A Indian Penal Code were not made out for the same reason as there was no evidence of cruelty and harassment to the deceased soon before her death. [21]

(ii) On a collective appreciation of the evidence led by the prosecution, this court was of the considered view that the prerequisites to raise presumption under Section 304B Indian Penal Code and Section 113B of the Indian Evidence Act having not been fulfilled, the conviction of the Appellant could not be justified. Mere death of the deceased being unnatural in the matrimonial home within seven years of marriage would not be sufficient to convict the Accused under Section 304B and 498A

Indian Penal Code. The cause of death as such was not known. [23]

Ratio Decidendi: Mere death of the deceased being unnatural in the matrimonial home within seven years of marriage will not be sufficient to convict the Accused under Section 304B and 498A Indian Penal Code.

Disposition: In Favour of Accused

Devender Singh and Ors. vs. The State of Uttarakhand (21.04.2022 - SC) : MANU/ SC/0517/2022

Relative Section:

Code of Criminal Procedure, 1973 (CrPC) - Section 313; Dowry Prohibition Act, 1961 - Section 2; Indian Evidence Act, 1872 - Section 113B; Indian Penal Code, 1860 (IPC) - Section 120B, Indian Penal Code, 1860 (IPC) - Section 302, Indian Penal Code, 1860 (IPC) - Section 304B, Indian Penal Code, 1860 (IPC) - Section 498A

Hon'bleJudges/Coram:

N.V. Ramana, C.J.I., A.S. Bopanna and Hima Kohli, JJ.

Equivalent Citation: 2022(235)AIC165, AIR2022SC2965, 2022 (2) ALD(Crl.) 367 (SC), 2022 (120) ACC 600, 2022CriLJ2545, 2022(2)Crimes277(SC), II(2022)DMC1SC, 2022(3)HLR256, 2022/INSC/ 457, 2022 (3)JKJ22[SC], 2022(3)KLT389, 2022(3)N.C.C.371, 2022(2)RCR(Criminal)816, 2022(2)RLW1482(SC)

NumberofPagesintheOriginalJudgment:10

Case Reference:

Bansi Lal v. State of Haryana MANU/SC/0051/2011; Maya Devi and Ors. v. State of Haryana MANU /SC/ 1398/2015; G.V. Siddaramesh v. State of Karnataka MANU/SC/0088/2010; Ashok Kumar v. State of Haryana MANU/SC/0491/2010

Case Note:

Criminal - Conviction - Legality - Section 498A, 304B and 120B of the Indian Penal Code, 1860 (IPC) and Section 113B of the Indian Evidence Act, 1872 - The Appellants have assailed the judgment passed by the High Court whereby the judgment passed by the learned Sessions Judge, acquitting them from the charges under Section 498A, 304B and 120B of the IPC - Whether in the facts and circumstances of the instant case, the Appellants No. 2 and 3 should also be held equally guilty as the Appellant No. 1?

Facts:

The Appellants have assailed the judgment passed by the High Court whereby the judgment passed by the learned Sessions Judge, acquitting them from the charges Under Section 498A, 304B and 120B of the IPC has been reversed and they have been sentenced to undergo rigorous imprisonment for a period of seven year with a fine of 10,000 and in default, to undergo simple imprisonment for three months for the offence under Section 304B of IPC. The Appellants have also been sentenced to undergo rigorous imprisonment for one year Under Section 120B of IPC and two years under Section 498A of IPC. Being aggrieved by the said judgment and order of conviction, the Appellants are before this Court, in this appeal by way of special leave.

Held, while allowing the appeal in part

1. Section 304B of IPC read along with Section 113B of the Act, 1872 makes it clear that once the prosecution has succeeded in demonstrating that a woman has been subjected to cruelty or harassment for or in connection with any demand for dowry soon after her death, a presumption shall be drawn against the said persons that they have caused dowry death as contemplated Under Section 304B of IPC. The said presumption comes with a rider as this presumption can be rebutted by the Accused on demonstrating during the trial that all the ingredients of Section 304B of IPC have not been satisfied. [11]

2. The deceased was residing at the matrimonial home and had gone missing in circumstances where all the ingredients of Section 304B stood satisfied, the evidence of Dr. Digvijay Singh (PW-10) becomes relevant. The nature of injuries found on the body of the deceased at the time of the post-mortem was adverted to and PW-10 has deposed that the death had occurred about a week earlier to the examination. He opined that death had occurred due to shock and blood flow from the injuries received before the death. The doctor was categorical that the cause of death was not from

drowning as there was no water inside the lungs and abdomen. Though learned Counsel for the Appellants referred to this aspect to contend that the High Court has erred in not properly considering the same, when it is indicated that the deceased had suffered injuries before her death and there was loss of blood and also when it is medically indicated that the death was not caused due to drowning as there was no water in her lungs and abdomen, the natural corollary and a fair conclusion would be that the said death had occurred even before falling into the river, which would Rule out any accidental fall, as sought to be claimed by the Appellants. In fact, this would only increase the burden cast upon the Appellants to explain the situation. [21]

3. Though, the Appellants have attempted to set up a story that the deceased had gone to hills to cut grass, as rightly noted by the High Court, she could not have gone alone. Be that as it may, except for a bald statement, the Appellants have not brought any material on record to demonstrate that it was a normal practice for the deceased to go to the hills for cutting grass more so in circumstances where she was less than six months at her matrimonial home, pregnant and also during that very period, she had been going to her parental house for continuing her education, as has been contended by the Appellants themselves. Therefore, in such a situation, the Appellants have miserably failed to rebut the presumption drawn against them under Section 113B of the Evidence Act, in a matter relating to an offence under Section 304B of Indian Penal Code. [22]

4. It is no doubt true that the evidence of PW-1 indicates that the deceased had informed her that the husband and the in-laws had been harassing her and when PW 1 had gone to drop her daughter back to the matrimonial home on 10th April, 2008, the in-laws had raised a dowry demand. However, what has also been brought on record is that the Appellants No. 2 and 3 were residing separately, in a different house. In the cross-examination of PW-1, a suggestion was made to her about the distance between the two houses. Further, fact remains that the trial Court also referred to this aspect in para 31 of the judgment where learned Counsel for the defence had brought to the notice of the Court that there were two ration cards and the ration card of the Appellants No. 2 and 3 is separate from that of the Appellant No. 1 which mentions his name and that of the deceased. That apart, the nature of the demand made was for a lumpsum amount of ` 2,00,000 or for constructing a house in Haridwar, either of which was essentially for the benefit of the Appellant No. 1.

Therefore, there is no specific role with regard to the demand of dowry and nor has any specific instance of cruelty and harassment been ascribed to the Appellants No. 2 and 3 except for the general assertion. Moreover, in a circumstance where the charge was also Under Section 120B Indian Penal Code, there is no specific evidence led by the prosecution relating to the conspiracy allegedly hatched by the Appellants. The Appellants No. 2 and 3 deserve to be given the benefit of doubt and their conviction would not be justified. [23]

5. The conviction and sentence handed down by the High Court to the Appellant No. 1 (husband of the deceased) is upheld. However, the conviction and sentence handed down by the High Court to the Appellants No. 2 and 3 is set aside. It is ordered that the Appellant No. 2 and 3 who were released on bail on 12th March, 2008, be set free. The bail bonds executed by the Appellants No. 2 and 3 are, accordingly, cancelled. Appellant No. 1 shall, however, surrender within two weeks and serve the remaining part of the sentence imposed on him. [24]

6. The appeal is partly allowed. [25]

Disposition: Appeal Partly Allowed

State of Madhya Pradesh vs. Jogendra and Ors. (11.01.2022 - SC) : MANU/SC/0027/ 2022

Relative Section:

Dowry Prohibition (Amendment) Act, 1984; Dowry Prohibition Act, 1961 - Section 2; Indian Evidence Act, 1872 - Section 113B, Indian Evidence Act, 1872 - Section 114; Indian Penal Code, 1860 (IPC) - Section 30, Indian Penal Code, 1860 (IPC) - Section 304B, Indian Penal Code, 1860 (IPC) - Section 306, Indian Penal Code, 1860 (IPC) - Section 498A

Hon'bleJudges/Coram:

N.V. Ramana, C.J.I. A.S. Bopanna and Hima Kohli, JJ

Equivalent Citation: 2022(231)AIC22, AIR2022SC933, 2022 (1) ALD(Crl.) 940 (SC), 2022 (119) ACC 317,2022 (1) ALT (Crl.) 390 (A.P.), 2022CriLJ1201, 2022(1)Crimes146(SC), 2022(3)CriminalCC446,III (2022)DMC140SC, 2022(1)HLR273, 2022/INSC/30, 2022(1)J.L.J.R.350, 2022(2)JKJ173[SC], 2022(1)JLJ307, 2022(1)KLJ635, 2022(2)N.C.C.525, 2022(1)PLJR304, 2022(1)RCR(Criminal)698, (2022)5SCC401, 2022 (1) SCJ 551, [2022]2SCR295

NumberofPagesintheOriginalJudgment: 11

Case Reference:

K. Prema S. Rao and Ors. v. Yadla Srinivasa Rao and Ors. MANU/SC/ 0890/2002; Appasaheb and Ors. v. State of Maharashtra MANU/SC/7002/ 2007; Rajinder Singh v. State of Punjab MANU/SC/0210/2015; Vipin Jaiswal (A-I) v. State of A.P. rep. by Pub. Prosecutor MANU/SC/0253/

2013; Bachni Devi and Ors. v. State of Haryana through Secretary, Home Department MANU/SC/0101/2011; Kulwant Singh and Ors. v. State of Punjab MANU/SC/0303/2013; Surinder Singh v. State of Haryana MANU/SC/1180/2013; Raminder Singh v. State of Punjab MANU/SC/0183/2014; Kans Raj v. State of Punjab and Ors. MANU/SC/0296/2000; Dinesh v. State of Haryana MANU/SC/0364/2014; Gurmeet Singh v. State of Punjab MANU/SC/0359/2021; Satbir Singh and Anr. v. State of Haryana MANU/SC/0361/2021; Sher Singh v. State of Haryana MANU/SC/0022/2015; Saro Rana and Ors. v. State of Jharkhand MANU/JH/0743/2004

Case Note:

Criminal - Conviction - Dowry death - Abatement of suicide - Sections 304B, 306, 498A of the Indian Penal Code, 1860 (IPC) - Trial Court convicted Accused 1 and 2 - High Court set aside conviction under abetment of suicide - Whether High Court erred in setting aside conviction as directed by Trial Court?

Facts:

The present appeal was preferred against the judgment whereby of conviction and sentence imposed on the original Accused No. 1/ husband of the deceased, and Accused No. 2/ father-in-law of the deceased was set aside under Sections 304-B and 306 of the IPC, while order of conviction maintained under Section 498-A of the IPC. Incase of Accused No. 2, conviction under Section 498-A was set aside. Hence, the present appeal.

Held, while partly allowing the Appeal:

Trial Court correctly interpreted the demand for money raised by the Respondents on the deceased for construction of a house as falling within the definition of the word "dowry". The Court must be sensitive to the social milieu from which the parties hail.[14]

The glairing circumstances when viewed together, can hardly mitigate the offence of the Respondents or take the case out of the purview of Section 304-B Indian Penal Code, when all the four pre-requisites for invoking the said provision stand satisfied, namely, that the death took place at her matrimonial home within seven years of her marriage; death took place in abnormal circumstances on account of burning and that too when she was five months pregnant; she had been subjected to cruelty and harassment by the Respondents soon before her death and such cruelty/ harassment was in connection with demand for dowry.[19]

No hesitation in holding that the analysis of the trial Court was correct and the Respondents deserved to be convicted under Sections 304-B and

498-A Indian Penal Code. Findings returned by the High Court that has acquitted the Respondents for the offence of abetment to commit suicide under Section 306 Indian Penal Code not disturbed, as the prosecution could not bring any conclusive evidence on record.[20]

Appeal partly allowed. [21]

Disposition: Appeal Partly Allowed

Jatinder Kumar vs. State of Haryana (17.12.2019 – SC) : MANU/SC/1755/2019

Relative Section:

Code of Criminal Procedure, 1973 (CrPC) - Section 313; Dowry Prohibition Act, 1961 - Section 2; Indian Evidence Act, 1872 - Section 113B; Indian Penal Code, 1860 (IPC) - Section 304B, Indian Penal Code, 1860 (IPC) - Section 306, Indian Penal Code, 1860 (IPC) - Section 406, 498A

Hon'bleJudges/Coram:

Deepak Gupta and Aniruddha Bose, JJ.

Equivalent Citation : AIR2020SC161, 2020 (1) ALD(Crl.) 563 (SC), 2020 (1) ALT (Crl.) 325 (A.P.),

2020 (1)Crimes1(SC),2020(1)CriminalCC181,
I(2020)DMC57SC,2020(1)HLR467,2019/INSC/1381,2020(1) JCC482 ,
2020(4)JKJ488[SC], 2020(I)OLR210, 2020(1)RCR(Criminal)479,
2019(17)SCALE772, (2020)16SCC721, 2019(3)UC2098

NumberofPagesintheOriginalJudgment: 7

Case Reference:

Appasaheb and Anr. v. State of Maharashtra MANU/SC/7002/2007; Union of India and others v. Garware Nylons Ltd. etc. MANU/SC/0967/ 1996; Chemical and Fibres of India Ltd. v. Union of India and others MANU/SC/0147/1997; Rajinder Singh v. State of Punjab MANU/SC/ 0210/2015

Case Note:

Criminal - Conviction - Legality - Sections 304-B and 498-A of Indian Penal Code, 1860 (IPC) and Section 313 of Code of Criminal Procedure,

1973 (CrPC) and Section 113B of Indian Evidence Act, 1872 - Conviction of Appellant under Section 306 of IPC was set aside but conviction and sentence on other counts were sustained, hence present appeal - Whether impugned order of conviction was liable to be set aside.

Facts:

The Appellant has been found to be guilty by the High Court, which finding affirms the judgment of the Trial Court convicting him for commission of offences under the provisions of Sections 304-B and 498-A of the IPC. The offences were related to suicidal death of his wife. The High Court, however, set aside his conviction under Section 306 of the IPC by the Trial Court. The Appellant was charged for subjecting his deceased wife to cruelty or harassment in connection with demand for dowry coupled with cruelty during the subsistence of her marriage during her stay in her matrimonial home. Charge was also framed against him for abetting Meenakshi's suicide. She had committed suicide in the night of 20th September 1991. Her marriage with the Appellant was solemnised on 7th March 1991. On 20th September 1991, the deceased victim had come to her parental home to attend "pagree ceremony" of a relative and ultimately returned to her matrimonial home along with the Appellant on that very evening. The mother and two brothers of the Appellant were also implicated with the same charges and convicted by the Trial Court. The High Court, however, acquitted them. Conviction of the Appellant under Section 306 of IPC was set aside but conviction and sentence on other counts were sustained. Main case of the Appellant argued by Senior Counsel that, there was no evidence of any torture for demand of dowry against the Appellant.

Held, while dismissing the appeal

1. The depositions of the prosecution witnesses about torture and demand for dowry made by the Appellant have been believed by the Trial Court as also the High Court. Barring the stray remark by P.W. 2, both P.W. 1 and P.W. 2 have narrated facts which would constitute demand for dowry as also inflicting cruelty and torture upon the deceased victim. Such consistent stand of these two witnesses cannot be said to have been overshadowed by the above-referred stray statement of P.W. 2 which is not in tune with rest of his deposition. As regards the Appellant, it is a finding on fact upon proper appreciation of evidence. There is no major contradiction in the statements made by P.W. 1 and P.W. 2 on demand for dowry and subjecting the deceased victim to cruelty. They stuck by

their statements in cross-examination. From their depositions, a link can be established between such acts of the Appellant and death of the deceased victim. Once these factors are proved, presumption rests on the Accused under Section 113B of Act, 1872. The Appellant in his statement made in response to his examination under Section 313 of the CrPC attributed suicide of the victim to depression on account of several of her relatives' deaths within a short spell of time. Though the factum of several deaths in her family has been established, there is no corroboration of such a depressive state of mind of the deceased. The other defence of the Appellant is that she was a modern urban lady and could not adjust to the life style of Mullana, a small town where her matrimonial home was situated. But both the Trial Court and the High Court rejected this defence. No reason to re-appreciate evidence on this aspect. Father of the deceased, as also P.W. 2 have proved the demand for dowry. This version has run consistently from the statement forming the basis of F.I.R. to deposition stage and we do not think the Trial Court and High Court had come to such conclusion in a perverse manner. [9]

4. It is also argument of the Appellant that since on the basis of same set of evidences, the co-Accused persons were acquitted, the Appellant only for the reason of being husband of the deceased could not be subjected to a different standard or yardstick in the guilt finding process. [10]

5. On the basis of the evidence on record, present Court is satisfied that, the judgment and order of conviction and sentence was rightly confirmed by the High Court so far as the Appellant is concerned. The factors which the High Court found for convicting the Appellant, establishes guilt of the Appellant beyond reasonable doubt. No reason to interfere with the judgment and order under appeal. The appeal is dismissed. [11]

Disposition: In Favour of State

CHAPTER NINETEEN

Kantilal vs. The State of Gujarat (04.10.2019 - SC) : MANU/SC/1393/2019

Relative Section:

Dowry Prohibition Act, 1961 - Section 3, Dowry Prohibition Act, 1961 - Section 7; Indian Penal Code, 1860 (IPC) - Section 114, Indian Penal Code, 1860 (IPC) - Section 149, Indian Penal Code, 1860 (IPC) - Section 306, Indian Penal Code, 1860 (IPC) - Section 323, Indian Penal Code, 1860 (IPC) - Section 498A

Hon'ble Judges/Coram:

L. Nageswara Rao and Hemant Gupta, JJ.

Equivalent Citation : 2020(209)AIC201, AIR2019SC4912, 2020 (1) ALD(Crl.) 39 (SC),

2020 (112) ACC 8,2019(3)ALT(Crl.)385(A.P.),2020(1)BLJ241,

2019(4)Crimes1(SC),2020(1)CriminalCC105,

III(2019)DMC44 7SC,2019(3)HLR782,2019/INSC/1134,2019(4)JCC4166,2019(5)JKJ47[SC],

2020(1)N.C.C.748, 2019(4) RCR (Criminal)809,

2020(1)RLW672(SC), 2019(13)SCALE566, (2019)9SCC603, 2019(3)UC1670

NumberofPagesintheOriginalJudgment: 4

Case Reference: nil

Case Note:

Criminal - Acquittal - Lack of evidence - Sections 114,149,306,323 and 498A of Indian Penal Code, 1860 and Sections 3 and 7 of Dowry Prohibition Act, 1961- FIR was registered under Sections 498A, 306, 323 and 149 of Code and Sections 3 and 7 of Act - On completion of investigation, charges were framed against all Accused - After conducting trial, Trial Court convicted all Accused under Sections 498A and 114 of Code - Accused No. 2 was further convicted under Section 306 of Code read with Sections 3 and 7 of Act - Accused No. 1 and Accused No. 3 were also convicted under Section 323 of Code - In Appeal filed by Accused, High Court acquitted Accused Nos. 3, 4 and 5, but upheld conviction of Accused No.1-Appellant for committing offences under Sections 498A, 114 and 323 of Code - Conviction and sentence of Accused No. 2 was also confirmed by High Court - Hence, present appeal - Whether impugned judgment of conviction against Appellant under Sections 498A,323 and 114 of Code was sustainable.

Facts:

FIR was registered under Sections 498A, 306, 323 and 149 of the Indian Penal Code, 1860 and Sections 3 and 7 of the Dowry Prohibition Act, 1961. On completion of the investigation, charges were framed against all the Accused. After conducting trial, the Trial Court convicted all the Accused under Sections 498A and 114 Indian Penal Code. Accused No. 2 was further convicted under Section 306 Indian Penal Code read with Sections 3 and 7 of the Dowry Prohibition Act. Accused No. 1-the Appellant and Accused No. 3 were also convicted under Section 323 of Code. In the Appeal filed by the Accused, the High Court acquitted Accused Nos. 3, 4 and 5, but upheld the conviction of the Appellant for committing offences under Sections 498A, 114 and 323 of Indian Penal Code. The conviction and sentence of Accused No. 2 -husband of the deceased, was also confirmed by the High Court.

Held, while allowing the appeal:

(i) Accused No. 2 who was the husband of the deceased accepted the conviction and served out the sentence imposed upon him and the conviction and sentence of Accused Nos. 3 and 5 were set aside. Apart from the allegation that the entire family harassed the deceased, the overt act attributed to the Appellant was that he had physically assaulted the deceased on two occasions. This allegation finds place in the FIR. Prosecution witness deposed in court about the Appellant beating the deceased on two occasions. Prosecution witness stated that he was informed by other witness about the incident of Appellant beating his deceased daughter. However, said witness did not speak of any such incident of the Appellant beating the deceased on two occasions. Reliance could not be placed on the sole testimony of prosecution witness, on the basis of which the Appellant was convicted under Sections 498A, 114 and 323 of Code as there was no corroboration by witness who was alleged to have given the information to him. Other than the above allegation, the Appellant stands on the same footing as of Accused Nos. 3, 4 and 5 who had been acquitted by the High Court. As the accusation of the physical assault by the Appellant on the deceased was not proved, he was entitled to be acquitted. [5]

(ii) Therefore, the Appellant was acquitted of the charges under Sections 498A, 114 and 323 of the Indian Penal Code. [6]

Disposition: In Favour of Accused

Sandeep Kumar and Ors. vs. State of Uttarakhand and Ors. (02.12.2020 - SC) : MANU/SC/0910/2020

Relative Section:

Code of Criminal Procedure, 1973 (CrPC) - Section 106, Code of Criminal Procedure, 1973 (CrPC) - Section 161, Code of Criminal Procedure, 1973 (CrPC) - Section 313, Code of Criminal Procedure, 1973 (CrPC) - Section 362, Code of Criminal Procedure, 1973 (CrPC) - Section 378, Code of Criminal Procedure, 1973 (CrPC) - Section 386; Dowry Prohibition Act, 1961 - Section 3, Dowry Prohibition Act, 1961 - Section 4; Indian Evidence Act, 1872 - Section 32, Indian Evidence Act, 1872 - Section 113A, Indian Evidence Act, 1872 - Section 113B; Indian Penal Code, 1860 (IPC) - Section 304B, Indian Penal Code, 1860 (IPC) - Section 306, Indian Penal Code, 1860 (IPC) - Section 498A

Hon'bleJudges/Coram:

Rohinton Fali Nariman, K.M. Joseph and Aniruddha Bose, JJ.

Equivalent   Citation:
2021(218)AIC107,AIR2021SC691,2021(1)ALD(Crl.)936(SC),2021(115)ACC342, 2020(4)Crimes508(SC),2021(2)CriminalCC277,I(2021)DMC92SC,2020/INSC/671,2020(6)JKJ1[SC],2020(4)   MLJ(Crl)667,   2021(1)N.C.C.85, 2021(3)RLW2072(SC), [2020]13SCR848, 2020(3)UC1963

NumberofPagesintheOriginalJudgment: 23
Case Reference:

Anant Chintaman Lagu v. The State of Bombay MANU/SC/0043/1959; Chhotan Sao and Ors. v. State of Bihar MANU/SC/1314/2013; Ghurey Lal v. State of U.P. MANU/SC/3223/2008; Sharad Birdhichand Sarda v. State of Maharashtra MANU/SC/0111/1984; Bhupinder Singh v. State of Punjab MANU/SC/0049/1988; Jaipal v. State of Haryana MANU/SC/0847/2002; Shanmughan v. State of Kerala MANU/SC/0052/2012; Bhupendra v. State of Madhya Pradesh MANU/SC/1159/2013; Anant Chintaman Lagu v. State of Bombay MANU /SC /0043/1959 : AIR 1960 SC 116; Subramanian v. Public Prosecutor 1956 (1) WLR 965

Case Note:

Criminal - Conviction - Section 304B of the Indian Penal Code, 1860 (IPC) - Impugned judgment reversed order of Acquittal - Prosecution alleged Appellant of causing dowry death of deceased - Death allegedly caused by poison - Appellant acquitted by Sessions Court for want of due evidence - High Court reversed the judgment to convict Appellants - Hence, the present appeal - Whether High Court vide impugned judgment rightly interfered with the reasoned findings directing acquittal?

Facts:

The Appellantswere charged with the offence punishable under Section 304B, IPC. They were acquitted by the Trial Court (Sessions Judge). The judgment of acquittal was however reversed in appeal filed by the complainant/Respondent No. 2and the Appellants after conviction under Section 304-B were sentenced to undergo imprisonment for life. As per the prosecution, deceased daughter of R2 was harassed by Appellants - her husband, father-in-law and mother-in-law for dowry. They were all alleged of killing her. The dead body was found in the car given to them in marriage. The death was caused by poison. Sessions Court while acquitting accused person held that prosecution was unable to prove that deceased died due to poison. Further no injury was also found on the body of the deceased as per the inquest report and post mortem. The oral evidence adduced ruled out physical cruelty in connection with the dowry. High Court in appeal held that the opinion of the doctor cannot affect the value of deposition of truthful eyewitness and Appellants also having failed to rebut the presumption under Section 113B of the Evidence Act. Prosecution held to have duly proved that the deceased was killed due to cruelty and harassment for dowry. Hence, the present appeal.

Held, while allowing the Appeals:

There is no evidence in this case which could have persuaded the High Court to conclude that there were compelling reasons to interfere with the acquittal by the High Court. The appreciation of the evidence of the witnesses by the trial court unless it is found to be a case of misreading of the evidence or are based on an erroneous understanding of the law, could not have been interfered with. [56]

Apart from the fact that prosecution has not been able to establish that the cause of death was unnatural, the case setup about the demand of Rs. 10 lakhs by Accused appears to be riddled with irreconcilable contradictions. Neither the post-mortem nor the Forensic Lab Report shows any poisoning. No poison has been recovered at all from the house of the Appellants. There are no marks of injury at all on the deceased. Even the material (wiper) recovered, according to prosecution, and which allegedly was used to clean vomit of the deceased, did not disclose any poison. Section 113B of Evidence Act may not apply in this case for the reason that in order that Section 113B applies, there must be evidence that soon before the death of the person, which proves that the person, who is alleged to have caused death, treated the deceased with cruelty or harassed her or in connection with a demand of dowry. [62]

The High Courtwithout any justification, reversed the acquittal. Appeals allowed. The impugned judgment of the High Court is set aside and the judgment of the Sessions Judge is restored. [63]

Disposition: In Favour of Accused

Arun Singh and Ors. vs. State of U.P. and Ors. (10.02.2020 - SC) : MANU/SC/0160/2020

Relative Section:

Code of Criminal Procedure, 1973 (CrPC) - Section 156(3), Code of Criminal Procedure, 1973 (CrPC) - Section 320, Code of Criminal Procedure, 1973 (CrPC) - Section 482; Dowry Prohibition Act, 1961 - Section 3, Dowry Prohibition Act, 1961 - Section 3(1), Dowry Prohibition Act, 1961 - Section 4, Dowry Prohibition Act, 1961 - Section 8(2); Indian Penal Code, 1860 (IPC) - Section 493

Hon'bleJudges/Coram:

Navin Sinha and Krishna Murari, JJ.

Equivalent   Citation   :
2020(213)AIC73,AIR2020SC1758,2020(2)ALD(Crl.)444(SC),
2020(113)ACC257, 2020(4)Crimes85(SC), 2020(1)HLR888, 2020/INSC/163, 2020(2)J.L.J.R.4,
2020(2)KLT83,   2020-2-LW   (Crl)   957,   2020(2)PLJR4, 2020(3)RLW2394(SC),
(2020)3SCC736, 2020 (5) SCJ 683, [2020]3SCR707

NumberofPagesintheOriginalJudgment:10

Case Reference:

Gian Singh v. State of Punjab and Anr. MANU/SC/0781/2012; Parbatbhai Aahir and Ors. v. State of Gujarat and Ors. MANU/SC/1241/2017; Narinder Singh and Ors. v. State of Punjab and Anr. MANU/SC/

0235/2014; Ram Chandra Bhagat v. State of Jharkhand MANU/SC/1024/ 2012; Amrawati and Anr. v. State of U.P. MANU /UP/0819/2004 : 2004 (57) ALR 290; Lal Kamlendra Pratap Singh v. State of U.P. MANU /SC /0449 /2009 : 2009 (3) ADJ 322 (SC)

Case Note:

Criminal - Quashing of proceedings - Section 493 of Indian Penal Code, 1860 and Section 3/4 of Dowry Prohibition Act, 1961 - Respondent No. 2 lodged First Information Report under Section 493 of Code read with Section 3/4 of Dowry Prohibition Act against Appellants - Matter was investigated and charge sheet was filed against Appellants, which was challenged before High Court by way of petition - High Court finding that there was no justification for quashing charge sheet dismissed petition - Hence, present appeal - Whether impugned criminal proceedings initiated against Appellants liable to be quashed.

Facts:

The Respondent No. 2 lodged First Information Report with Police Station under Section 493 Indian Penal Code read with Section 3/4 of the Dowry Prohibition Act against the Appellants. The matter was investigated by the concerned Police Station and a charge sheet was filed against the Appellants, which was challenged before the High Court by way of petition under Section 482 Code of Criminal Procedure. The High Court finding that there was no justification for quashing the charge sheet dismissed the petition.

Held, while partly allowing the appeal:

(i) To constitute an offence under Section 493 Indian Penal Code, the allegations in the FIR must demonstrate that Appellant had practiced deception on the daughter of the complainant causing a false belief of existence of lawful marriage and which led her to cohabit with him. [22]

(ii) From a perusal of the F.I.R., there was no allegations made therein could be said to constitute any offence under Section 493 Indian Penal Code. There were no allegation of any inducement or any deceit to make the victim believe that she was lawfully married to the Appellant, which mislead her to have sexual intercourse with the Accused Appellant No. 1. Only allegations in the First Information Report in this regard were that after the marriage was settled, the Appellant No. 1 started visiting the house of the complainant frequently and would mislead and instigate his daughter that relation is final and only Feras remains to be performed. On the fateful day, the Appellant No. 1 took leave and enticed and instigated his daughter took her to his room and promising that she was being his wife established physical relations. [23]

(iii) A perusal of the averments would go to show that ingredients to constitute an offence under Section 493 Indian Penal Code are missing from the averments. The allegations did not even prima-facie, cull out any inducement of belief in the victim that she was lawfully married to the Appellant No. 1 and on account of this deceitful misstatement, the victim co-habited with the Accused. Since the essential ingredients to constitute an offence under Section 493 Indian Penal Code were missing from the allegations made in the F.I.R., offence under the said Section could not be said to be made out against the Appellants. [24]

(iv) A reading of the Section 3/4 of Act shows that essential ingredients of the offence under Section 3/4 of the Dowry Prohibition Act are that the persons Accused should have made demand directly or indirectly from the parents or other relatives or guardians of a bride or a bridegroom as the case may be any dowry and/or abets the giving and taking of dowry. The allegations of the F.I.R. quoted hereinabove clearly go to show that a demand of dowry was made by the Appellants from the complainants and thus it could not be said that no offence under the Dowry Prohibition Act are made out against the Appellants. There being direct allegations of demand of Dowry in the First Information Report, the allegations prima-facie constitute a commission of an offence under the Dowry Prohibition Act and thus the charges leveled against the Appellants under Section 3/4 of the said Act, were not liable to be quashed. [29]

Disposition: In Favour of State

Adv. Jayprakash Somani's Videos On Law

Adv. Jayprakash Somani's Videos on Law on Youtube- 'jaysomani64' channel.

1) SLP in Supreme Court / Special Leave Petitions in the Supreme Court of India

2) Transfer of Civil & Criminal Cases by the Supreme Court of India / Transfer of Matrimonial Cases

3) Appellate Jurisdiction of the Supreme Court of India

4) Jurisdictions of the Supreme Court of India

5) Public Interest Litigation in the Supreme Court of India / PIL in Supreme Court

6) Article 32 Writ Petitions in the Supreme Court of India

7) Bail Matters Top 10 Supreme Court Cases

8) FIR Quashing in High Court & Supreme Court

9) Bail & Anticipatory Bail Matters in Supreme Court

10) Insolvency & Bankruptcy Matters in the Supreme Court

11) Insolvency & Bankruptcy Code 2016 Part 1

12) Insolvency & Bankruptcy Code 2016 Part 2

13) Insolvency & Bankruptcy Code 2016 Part 3

14) Corporate Liquidation Process

15) Supreme Court Rules & Procedures Webinar of 2.5 hour on Zoom

16) RDDBFI Act, 1993 (Introduction)

17) The Indian Contact Act 1872

18) Negotiable Instruments Act (Introduction)

19) How to avoid matrimonial disputes& some more videos

20) SEBI Matters in the Supreme Court

21) Matrimonial Matters: Supreme Court's 20 Case Laws

22) Consumer Matters Supreme Court's 20 Case Laws

23) Service Matters Supreme Court's 20 Case Laws

24) How to Search Lawyer for Your Matter

25) Property Matters Supreme Court's 20 Case Laws

26) Bail Matters: Supreme Court's 20 Case Laws

27) Supreme Court / High Court Vacation Benches

28) 69000 Teacher's Recruitment Matters of UP Government in the Supreme Court

29) Contempt of Court Matters in the Supreme Court

30) Advocate Act's Matters in the Supreme Court

31) Business Law Matters in the Supreme Court

32) Banking Matters in the Supreme Court

33) Labour Law Matters in the Supreme Court

34) Arbitration Matters in the Supreme Court

35) Careers in Law -Zoom Webinar by Adv. Jayprakash Somani

36) Civil Matters in the Supreme Court

37) Consumer Protection Act | Consumer Matters in the Supreme Court

38) Corporate Matters in the Supreme Court

39) Criminal Matters in the Supreme Court

40) Role of Respondent in the Supreme Court of India

41) Motor Vehicle Accident Matters in Supreme Court with case laws

42) Article 131 Original Suits in Supreme Court

43) PIL in Supreme Court/ Public Interest Litigations in the Supreme Court of India'

44) CAB Citizenship Amendment Bill is not Unconstitutional

45) Supreme Court of India Cases & Process – Marathi

46) Legal Services Export / Export of Legal Services

47) Transfer of Matrimonial Cases by the Supreme Court of India

48) Public Interest Litigation PIL

49) The Specific Relief Act (Introduction)

50) Corporate Insolvency Resolution Process CIRP

51) ABMM's Career 5 - Careers in Law

52) Transfer of cases by Supreme Court

53) Writ Petitions in High Court & Supreme Court of India

54) Supreme Court Jurisdictions - Appeals, SLP, Writ Petitions, Transfer, Original, Review, Curative

55) LEGAL INDIA TV Show: Cases Handled in Supreme Court

56) Corporate Liquidation Process

57) Legal Services Export / Export of Legal Services

58) Corporate Laws

59) Election Matters- Supreme Court's 20 Case Laws

60) Companies Act, 2013

62) Competition Act, 2002

63) Banking Matters - Supreme Court's 20 Case Laws

64) Election Matters in the Supreme Court

65) Armed Forces Tribunal Matters in the Supreme Court

66) Compassionate Appointment Service matter

67) Foreign Exchange Management Act FEMA

68) Foreign Trade Policy 2021-26 Proposed

69) Customs Act 1962

70) Narcotic Drugs and Psychotropic Substances Act, 1985 NDPS Act

71) Foreign Trade Development & Regulation Act, 1992

72) How to Search Good Advocate in the Supreme Court of India

73) Sr. Adv Vikas Singh's Interview in Nani Palkhivala Wednesday Law Club

74) Indian Penal Code (I. P. C.)

75) Criminal Procedure Code (Cr. P. C.)

76) Commercial Courts & International Arbitration - by Mr. Jaideep Gupta, Senior Advocate in Nani Palkhivala Wednesday Law Club

77) Sr. Adv Ranji Thomos in Nani Palkhivala Wednesday Law Club

78) Urgent Matters in Supreme Court during vacations

79) 498A Bail Matters in Supreme Court

81) 376 Bail Matters in Supreme Court

82) 302, 304, 307, 308 Bail Matters in Supreme Court

83) 138, 420 Bail Matters in Supreme Court

84) POCSO Act Bail Matters in Supreme Court

85) NDPS Act Bail Matters in Supreme Court

86) What is ED (Enforcement Directorate)?

87) Prevention of Money Laundering Act, 2002 (PMLA Act)

88) Insolvency & Bankruptcy Code- Supreme Court Case Laws. Webinar in Nani Palkhivala Wednesday Law Club

89) What is NCLT & NCLAT?

90) Acquittal from 376 Supreme Court's some case laws in Nani Palkhivala Wednesday Law Club dt 28.7.22

91) Insolvency & Bankruptcy in India

92) Can we file case directly in the Supreme Court?

93) Adv. Anuja Pethia has cleared AOR Exam 2021 with 77% marks - Her interview in Nani Palkhivala Wednesday Law Club

94) Customs Act - Supreme Court Case Laws & Interview of AOR Adv. Anuja Pethia in Nani Palkhivala Law Club.

95) The Uttar Pradesh Public Service Tribunals Act, 1976

96) POCSO Act - Supreme Court Case Laws & Interview of AOR Adv. Shoumendu Mukharji & Adv. Nishant Verma in Nani Palkhivala Law Club.

97) Who Can Trigger CIRP Process Under Insolvency Law of India

98) The Uttar Pradesh Government Servant Discipline and Appeal Rules, 1999

99) CIRP Application Under Sec 7 by FC

100) Information Technology Act 2000

101) Uttar Pradesh Recruitment of Dependants of Government Servants Dying in Harness Rules, 1974

102) Foreign Exchange Management Act 1999 & Supreme Court's Case Laws on FEMA & Leading Case of AOR Exam in Nani Palkhivala Law Club.

103) Arbitration and Conciliation Act 1996 & It's Supreme Court Case Laws in Nani Palkhivala Wednesday Law Club.

104) Narcotic Drugs & Psychotropic Substances Act 1985 (NDPS Act) & It's Supreme Court Case Laws in Nani Palkhivala Wednesday Law Club.

105) Recovery of Debts and Bankruptcy Act 1993

106) Uttar Pradesh Land Revenue Code 2006

107) CIRP Application Under Sec 9 by OC

108) CIRP Application Under Sec 10 by CD

109) Hindu Succession Act, 1956

110) Maharashtra Civil Services Rules, 1981

111) Indian Contract Act, 1872 & Supreme Court's Case Laws" in Nani Palkhiwala Wednesday Law Club

112) Securities and Exchange Board of India Act, 1992 i. e. SEBI Act 1992 & Case Laws on Insiders Trading" in Nani Palkhiwala Wednesday Law Club

113) Moratorium Under Section 14 of IBC, 2016

114) Hindu Marriage Act, 1955

115) Maharashtra Land Revenue Code, 1966

116) 64 Leading Cases of AOR Exam Session 1 :- Cases 1 to16 in Nani Palkhiwala Wednesday Law Club

117) 64 Leading Cases of AOR Exam Session 2: Cases 17 to 32 in Nani Palkhiwala Wednesday Law Club

118) 64 Leading Cases of AOR Examination Session 3: Cases 33 to 48 in Nani Palkhivala Wednesday Law Club

119) 64 Leading Cases of AOR Exam Session 4: Cases 49 to 64 in Nani Palkhiwala Wednesday Law Club

120) Labour Laws of India: Part 1 - 4 New Labour Law Codes of India

121) New Labour Laws Part 2 The Code on Wages, 2019

122) New Labour Laws Part 3:- The Code on Social Security, 2020

123) Argue in English Fluently & Confidently - Two months online course.

124) SLP Admission in the Supreme Court. 2023 (Hindi)

125) Transfer of Petitions from the Supreme Court (Hindi)

126) Review Petition in the Supreme Court.(Hindi)

127) Recovery of debts from the Company (Hindi)

128) How to search 'Good Insolvency & Bankruptcy Consultant?' (HINDI)

129) Curative Petition in the Supreme Court

130) AFT Appeals in the Supreme Court (HINDI)

131) NCLAT's Appeals in the Supreme Court.

132) Transfer Petition: Which matters can we transfer?

133) SLP Types of SLP in the Supreme court of India (English).

134) Argue in English Fluently and Confidently in the High Court & Supreme Court'

List Of Adv. Jayprakash Somani's Published Books

1. Supreme Court of India's Leading Case Laws on 'Insolvency & Bankruptcy Code 2016'

2. Bail Matters – Supreme Court's Latest Leading Case Laws

3. Arbitration Matters- Supreme Court's Latest Leading Case Laws

4. Property Matters - Supreme Court's Latest Leading Case Laws

5. Matrimonial Matters- Supreme Court's Latest Leading Case Laws

6. Election Matters- Supreme Court's Latest Leading Case Laws

7. SEBI Matters- Supreme Court's Latest Leading Case Laws

8. Banking Matters- Supreme Court's Latest Leading Case Laws

9. Service Matters- Supreme Court's Latest Leading Case Laws

10. Contempt of Court Matters- Supreme Court's Latest Leading Case Laws

11. Consumer Protection Matters- Supreme Court's Latest Leading Case Laws

12. Corporate Law- Supreme Court's Latest Leading Case Laws

13. Supreme Court's AOR Exam- Leading Cases

14. Armed Force Tribunal - Supreme Court's Latest Leading Case Laws

15. Acquittal From 376 - Supreme Court's Latest Leading Case Laws

16. Negotiable instrument – Supreme Court's Latest Leading Case Laws

17. Contract Act- Supreme Court's Latest Leading Case Laws

18. Insider trading- Supreme Court's Latest Leading Case Laws

19. Foreign Exchange and Management Act- Supreme Court's Latest Leading Case Laws

20. Income Tax Act- Supreme Court's Latest Leading Case Laws

21. Company Law- Supreme Court's Latest Leading Case Laws

22. Competition & Monopoly Matters- Supreme Court's Latest Leading Case Laws

23. Compassionate Appointment- Service Matters- Supreme Court's Latest Leading Case Laws

24. Compulsory Retirement- Service Matters- Supreme Court's Latest Leading Case Laws

25. Voluntary Retirement- Service Matters- Supreme Court's Latest Leading Case Laws

26. Removal/Dismissal/Termination from Service- Supreme Court's Latest Leading Case Laws

27. Seniority- Service Matter- Supreme Court's Latest Leading Case Laws

28. Promotion- Service Matter- Supreme Court's Latest Leading Case Laws

29. Equal Pay for Equal Work- Service Matter- Supreme Court's Latest Leading Case Laws

30. Condition of Service- Service Matter- Supreme Court's Latest Leading Case Laws

31. Customs Act- Supreme Court's Leading Case Laws

32. Information Technology Act- Supreme Court's Leading Case Laws

33. SEC. 125 CR. P. C.- Supreme Court's Leading Case Laws

34. SEC. 498A OF I. P. C.- Supreme Court's Leading Case Laws

35. MOTOR VEHICLE ACT- Supreme Court's Leading Case Laws

36. CONDITION OF SERVICE- SERVICE MATTER- Supreme Court's Leading Case Laws

37. SUSPENSION- SERVICE MATTER- Supreme Court's Leading Case Laws

38. Reservation in SC, ST, OBC- Service Matter- Supreme Court's Leading Case Laws

39. NARCOTIC DRUGS AND PSYCHOTROPIC SUBSTANCES (NDPS) ACT - Supreme Court of India's Latest Leading Case Laws

40. SEC 302 IPC - Supreme Court of India's Latest Leading Case Laws

41. PROTECTION OF CHILDREN FROM SEXUAL OFFENCES ACT (POCSO) - Supreme Court of India's Latest Leading Case Laws

42. PMLA ACT BAIL MATTERS - Supreme Court of India's Leading Case Laws

43. SEC 376 BAIL MATTERS - Supreme Court of India's Leading Case Laws

44. SEC 302 BAIL MATTERS - Supreme Court of India's Leading Case Laws

45. POCSO ACT BAIL MATTERS - Supreme Court of India's Leading Case Laws

46. JUVENILE JUSTICE ACT- Supreme Court of India's Leading Case Laws

47. TRANSFER OF PROPERTY ACT- Supreme Court of India's Leading Case Laws

48. PROFESSIONAL ETHICS OF ADVOCATES- AOR EXAM- SUPREME COURT'S LEADING CASE LAWS

49. WHITE COLLAR CRIME- SUPREME COURT'S LEADING CASE LAWS

50. SEC 302 BAIL MATTERS- SUPREME COURT'S LEADING CASE LAWS

51. SEC 7 IBC 2016 - SUPREME COURT'S LATEST LEADING CASE LAW

52. ADVERSE POSSESSION IN PROPERTY MATTER - SUPREME COURT'S LATEST LEADING CASE LAWS

53. FOOD SAFETY AND STANDARD ACT 2006' - SUPREME COURT AND HIGH COURT's LEADING CASE LAWS

54. ARMED FORCE TRIBUNAL ACT- SUPREME COURT'S LATEST LEADING CASE LAWs

55. ESSENTIAL COMMODITIES ACT 1955- SUPREME COURT'S LATEST LEADING CASE LAWS

56. 'FOREIGN TRADE DEVELOPMENT AND REGULATION ACT'- SUPREME COURT AND HIGH COURT'S LEADING CASE LAWS

57. 'PARTNERSHIP ACT 1932'- SUPREME COURT'S LEADING CASE LAWS

58. 'COTPA ACT 2003' - SUPREME COURT AND HIGH COURT'S LEADING CASE LAWS

59. DOMESTIC VIOLENCE ACT 2005' - SUPREME COURT'S LEADING CASE LAWS

Books are available online in India

1. Notion Press: https://notionpress.com/author/jayprakash_somani

2. Amazon: https://www.amazon.in/s?k=jayprakash+somani

3. Flipkart: https://www.flipkart.com/search?q=Jayprakash%20Somani

Books are available online at International Market

4. Amazon International: https://www.amazon.com/s?k=jayprakash+somani

5. Amazon United Kingdom: https://www.amazon.co.uk/s?k=jayprakash+somani

6. E-Books/Kindle edition at National & International Level: https://www.amazon.in/s?k=jaypraksh+somani

Adv Jayprakash Somani's Online Courses

Download our app to get access to our Free Videos, Free Bare Acts, Free Study Material in Legal as well as International Business Regime.

Android App Link ;-https://clpandrea.page.link/cmSm

Ios APp Link :-https://apps.apple.com/us/app/classplus/id1324522260

Login with org code ;- (qywzji)

Web Link ;-https://qywzji.courses.store/

Download App on Google play store - Type

Jayprakash Somani SupremeCourt

Legal Courses :

1. SLP- Bail Matters- Drafting & Successful Arguing in the Supreme Court.

Description - This Course is helpful to Advocates, Litigants, Law Officers, Law Students, Law Schools, Individual. Course contains 8 Videos + Study Material+ PDF Books. Access to this course is for Two Years. Expected duration of this course is one month only.

Topics : 1. SLP- Bail Matters- Drafting & Successful Arguing in the Supreme Court, **2.** Types of bails, **3.** Laws related to bail matters, **4.** How to read Impugned Order of High Court & frame substantial question of laws, **5.** How to draft excellent SLP, **6.** Searching of citations/ case laws, **7.** How to argue in admission hearings, **8.** How argue in after notice hearing.

Speaker: Jayprakash Bansilal Somani, MBA (Foreign Trade), LL. B. Advocate, Supreme Court of India & IP www.jayprakashsomani.com Call: P. A. 9322188701

2. SLP- Succession Matters- Drafting & Successful Arguing in the Supreme Court.

Description - This Course is helpful to Advocates, Litigants, Law Officers, Law Students, Law Schools, Individual. Course contains 9 Videos + Study Material+ PDF Books. Access to this course is for Two Years. Expected duration of this course is one month only.

Topics :1. SLP- Succession Matters- Drafting & Successful Arguing in the Supreme Court, **2.** Information about Succession Matters, **3.** Laws related to Succession Matters, **4.** How to read Impugned Order of High Court to frame substantial questions of law, **5.** How to draft excellent synopsis & list of date, **6.** Drafting of SLP of Succession Matter, **7.** Searching of citations/ case laws, **8.** How to prepare notes & then argue in admission hearings, **9.** How to prepare notes & then argue in after notice final hearing.

Speaker: Jayprakash Bansilal Somani, MBA (Foreign Trade), LL. B. Advocate, Supreme Court of India & IP www.jayprakashsomani.com Call: P. A. 9322188701

3. Legal Vocabulary & its practice pattern to Argue in High Court and Supreme Court / Improve Your Legal English

Description - This Course is helpful to Advocates, Litigants, Law Officers, Law Students, Law Schools, Individual. Course contains 11 Videos + Study Material+ PDF Books. Access to this course is for Two Years. Expected duration of this course is three month only.

Topics : 1. Legal Vocabulary & its practice pattern to Argue in High Court and Supreme Court / Improve Your Legal English, **2.** 1000 legal verbs with its three forms, **3.** Twelve Tenses with its running practice, **4.** One Pdf book on legal vocabulary & its practice pattern with Latin Terms, **5.** Second Pdf book on legal vocabulary & its practice pattern with Latin Terms, **6.** Some Videos of CJI Dr. Dhananjay Chandrachud for the practice of good legal English, **7.** Some Video/Audio Lectures of Legend Nani Palkhivala for standard perfect legal English & flow of Speech, **8.** Some Videos of renowned Sr. Advocates from Mumbai for flow, legal vocabulary & their struggle in legal journey, **9.** Some Videos of Sr. Advocates of the Supreme Court for flow & legal vocabulary, **10.** Some Videos of foreign persons to improve Professional English & thinking process in English, **11.**

Some important legal doctrines with case laws.

Speaker: Jayprakash Bansilal Somani, MBA (Foreign Trade), LL. B. Advocate, Supreme Court of India & IP www.jayprakashsomani.com Call: P. A. 9322188701.

4. SLP- Property Matters - Drafting and Successful Arguing in the Supreme Court.

Description - This Course is helpful to Advocates, Litigants, Law Officers, Law Students, Law Schools 8 Individual. Course contains 9 Videos + Study Material+ PDF Books. Access to this course is for Two Years. Expected duration of this course is one month only.

Topics : 1. SLP- Property Matters - Drafting and Successful Arguing in the Supreme Court, **2.** Types of Property Matters, **3.** Laws related to Property Matters, **4.** How to read Impugned Order of High Court to guide client & frame substantial question of laws, **5.** How to draft Synopsis & List of Dates in Property Matter, **6.** How to draft excellent SLP of Property Matter, **7.** Searching of citations/ case laws with specific paras, **8.** How to argue confidently in admission hearings, **9.** How argue confidently in after notice & final hearings.

Speaker: Jayprakash Bansilal Somani, MBA (Foreign Trade), LL. B. Advocate, Supreme Court of India & IP www.jayprakashsomani.com Call: P. A. 9322188701.

International Business Courses -
1. Agri Products Exports - Scope from India.

Description - This Course is helpful to Agriculturalists, Entrepreneurs, Exporters, Importers, Students. Course contains 12 Videos + Study Material+ PDF Books. Access to this course is for Two Years. Expected duration of this course is one month only.

Topics : **1**- Agri Products Exports - Scope from India, **2.** Agri Export's share in India's total export, **3.** Agri Export Promotional Council's Support, **4.** Top 10 Agri export countries, **5.** Top 10 Agri export product, **6.** India's share in World's Agri Exports, **7.** Onion Exports from India, **8.** Rice Exports from India, **9.** Mango Exports from India, **10.** Fresh Vegetable Exports, **11.** Fresh Fruits Exports, **12.** Export of Agri Allied Products.

Speaker: Jayprakash Bansilal Somani, MBA (Foreign Trade), LL. B. Advocate, Supreme Court of India & IP www.jayprakashsomani.com Call: P. A. 9322188701.

2. Textile Exports - Scope from India.

Description - This Course is helpful to Textile Business Houses, Entrepreneurs, Exporters, Importers, Students. Course contains 14 Videos + Study Material+ PDF Books. Access to this course is for Two Years. Expected duration of this course is one month only.

Topics : 1- Textile Exports - Scope from India, **2.** Textile Export's share in India's total exports, **3.** Support of Textile Export Promotional Council, **4.** Top 10 Countries in Textile Exports, **5.** Top 10 Products in Textile Exports, **6.** Export of Readymade Garments, **7.** Export of Man-made Textiles, **8.** Export of Handloom Products, **9.** Export of Wool & Woollen Textiles, **10.** Export of Silk, **11.** Exports of Handicrafts & Carpets, **12.** Exports of Coir & Coir Manufacturers, **13.** Exports of Jute,14. India's share in World's total textile expor.

Speaker: Jayprakash Bansilal Somani, MBA (Foreign Trade), LL. B. Advocate, Supreme Court of India & IP www.jayprakashsomani.com Call: P. A. 9322188701.

3. Export Import Procedure -Perfect Documentation & It's Management.

Description -This Course is helpful to Business Men, Service Providers, Entrepreneurs, Exporters, Importers, Students. Course contains 13 Videos + Study Material+ PDF Books. Access to this course is for Two Years. Expected duration of this course is three months only.

Topics : 1. Export Import Procedure, Perfect Documentation & Its management, **2.** Company Formation, **3.** Opening of Bank Account in AD Bank, **4.** Export Procedure points, **5.** Import Procedure Points, **6.** Taking Import Export Code, **7.** Taking RCMC number, **8.** Registration at Port when necessary, **9.** Quality Inspection Certificate of Goods, **10.** CHA & its roll, **11.** Custom Formalities, **12.** Export Documents such as Invoice, Bill of Lading, Insurance Certificate, Quality Inspection Certificate & others, **13.** Excellent Management of Export & Imports Documents.

Speaker: Jayprakash Bansilal Somani, MBA (Foreign Trade), LL. B. Advocate, Supreme Court of India & IP www.jayprakashsomani.com Call: P. A. 9322188701.

4. Jewellery Exports -Scope from India

Description - You can understand world wide scope for Jems & Jewellery in multidimensional ways. 14 videos of this course will create positive spark among you to enter into the Exports & Imports of Gems & Jewellery and other products. Chance to ask your query to Somani Sir every week.

Topics :1. Jewellery Exports - Scope from India, **2.** Jewellery Export's share in India's total exports, **3.** Support of Jems & Jewellery Export Promotional Council, **4.** Top 10 Countries in Jewellery Exports, **5.** Top 10 Products in Jewellery Exports, **6.** Export of Cut & Polished Diamonds, **7.** Export of Gold Jewellery, **8.** Export of Plain Gold Jewellery, **9.** Export of Studded Gold Jewellery, **10.** Export of Silver Jewellery, **11.** Exports of Platinum Jewellery, **12.** Exports of Imitation Jewellery, **13.** Exports of Articles of Gold, Silver & others, **14.** India's share in World's total Jewellery export.

Speaker: Jayprakash Bansilal Somani, MBA (Foreign Trade), LL. B. Advocate, Supreme Court of India & IP www.jayprakashsomani.com Call: P. A. 9322188701.

5. Export Import Finance Management with LC, ECGC & Venture Capital.

Description -You can understand A to Z about International Finance with LC, ECGC & Venture Capital in simple language & with illustrations. 11 videos of this course will create positive spark among you regarding International Finance Management with practical tips. Chance to ask your query to Somani Sir every week.

Topics : 1. Export Import Finance Management with LC, ECGC & Venture Capital, **2.** Which is good & excellent source of finance, **3.** Banking Finance, **4.** List of Banks which provides finance for International Business, **5.** How to start business in Less or Zero Capital, **6.** Letter of Credit, **7.** Types of LCs **8.** Scrutiny of L/C, **9.** ECGC Policy, **10.** Venture Capital Finance., **11.** Ideal formula of Investment & continues growth.

Speaker: Jayprakash Bansilal Somani, MBA (Foreign Trade), LL. B. Advocate, Supreme Court of India & IP www.jayprakashsomani.com Call: P. A. 9322188701.

6. Shipping & Logistics in International Business with live links of Ports, ICDs, CHAs etc.

Description - This Course is helpful to any Businessman, Professionals, Entrepreneurs, Exporters, Importers, CHAs, & Students.

Course contains following 10 Videos + Study Material+ PDF Books. Access to this course is for Two Years. Expected duration of this course is three months only.

Topics : 1. Shipping & Logistics in International Business with live links of Ports, ICDs, CHAs etc, **2.** Roll of CHA in Shipping & Logistics of International Business, **3.** How to find good & genuine CHA, **4.** Courier/

post service for small parcel, **5.** India's important Ports & ICDs with live links, **6.** How & what to study Ports/ ICDs websites, **7.** Art to reduce charges of Shipping & logistics, **8.** Information about some Top International Ports with live links, **9.** Roll of Customs in Exports & Imports,**10.** How to become CHA .

Speaker: Jayprakash Bansilal Somani, MBA (Foreign Trade), LL. B. Advocate, Supreme Court of India & IP www.jayprakashsomani.com Call: P. A. 9322188701.

7. International Business Marketing Part 1: Finding Potential & Genuine Buyers for Exports and Suppliers for Imports.

Description -You can understand Seven Excellent ways to Find Potential & Genuine Buyers for Exports and Suppliers for Imports with illustrations. 11 videos of this course will create positive spark among you regarding International Business Marketing with practical tips. Chance to ask your query to Somani Sir every week.

Topics : 1. International Business Marketing Part 1: Finding Potential & Genuine Buyers for Exports and Suppliers for Imports,**2.** Seven Excellent Ways to find Potential Buyers for Exports, **3.** Top 20 B to B Websites in the World, **4.** Searching Potential Buyers from B to B Sites. Is this safe & good way to search potential buyers, **5.** Searching Potential Buyers through Export Promotional Councils & Its Magazines, **6.** Searching Potential Buyers with help from Embassies, **7.** Searching Potential Buyers through Chamber of Commerce at global level, **8.** Searching Potential Buyers from International Trade Fairs & Exhibitions, **9.** Searching Potential Buyers through your friends & relatives or any Indian Person in focus countries, **10.** How to find focus countries for your products or services, **11.** Taking references from establish buyer/seller.

Speaker: Jayprakash Bansilal Somani, MBA (Foreign Trade), LL. B. Advocate, Supreme Court of India & IP www.jayprakashsomani.com Call: P. A. 9322188701.

8. International Business Marketing Part 2: Communication Skill to take repeated orders from Potential Buyers

Description - You can learn Perfect Communication Skills to initiate International Trade with foreign buyers and art to take repeated orders from these Potential Buyers with illustrations. 11 videos of this course will create positive spark among you to reach upto One Star Exporter Level rapidly and subsequent journey to reach upto Five Star Export House. Chance to ask your query to Somani Sir every week.

Topics :1. International Business Marketing Part 2: Communication Skill to take repeated orders from Potential Buyers,**2.** Preparation of Impressive Company Profile, **3.** Excellent Product CatLog for International Market, **4.** Phone Calls with maintaining dignity of ourself & our country, **5.** Sending emails, **6.** Sending what's app messages, **7.** Technique of repeated follow up, **8.** Art of taking 100% advance payments, **9.** Before giving credit facility how to look credibility of potential buyers or suppliers, **10.** Art of earning good profit of margin, **11.** Art of managing international clients.

Speaker: Jayprakash Bansilal Somani, MBA (Foreign Trade), LL. B. Advocate, Supreme Court of India & IP www.jayprakashsomani.com Call: P. A. 9322188701.